Elementary Music Theory

Mark Sarnecki

San Marco Publications

Book 2

Elementary Music Theory © 2023 by San Marco Publications. All rights reserved.

All right reserved. No part of this book may be reproduced in any form or by electronic or mechanical means including Information storage and retrieval systems without permission in writing from the author.

ISNB: 9781896499017

Contents

Franz Schubert	4
Review of Notes and Rests	5
Measures	6
Robert Schumann	11
The Grand Staff Review	12
Note Stems	15
Review Quiz 1	18
Johannes Brahms	21
Half Steps and Whole Steps	22
Sharps	23
Flats	26
Sharps and Flats on White Keys	31
Natural	33
Accidentals	35
Frédéric Chopin	41
Intervals	42
Review Quiz 2	47
Pyotr Il'yich Tchaikovsky	51
Major Scales	52
Key Signatures	56
Review Quiz 3	68

Franz Schubert
(1797-1828)

Schubert was born in Vienna, Austria. His whole family was musical, and Schubert received his earliest lessons at home. His father, who was also a schoolmaster, taught him violin. His older brother Ignaz taught him piano.

Schubert's beautiful voice won him a place in the Imperial Choir School. There he continued his music studies until the age of sixteen. After that, he taught for a few years in his father's school, and spent all his spare time making music. In 1818, he decided to devote himself entirely to music.

In the remaining years of his life, he wrote symphonies, operas, chamber music, piano works, church music, and over 600 songs. Schubert wrote short pieces with one movement of the pen across the paper...he rarely made corrections! Sometimes he wrote as many as eight songs in one day. These he presented to his friends at informal music gatherings.

Review of Notes and Rests

Fill in the blanks below.

Name	Note/Rest	Beats
whole note	𝅝	4
	♪	
	𝄺	
	♩	
	𝄾	
	𝄻	
	𝄼	
	𝅗𝅥	
	𝅗𝅥.	
	♫	

5

Measures

The staff is divided by bar lines into measures.

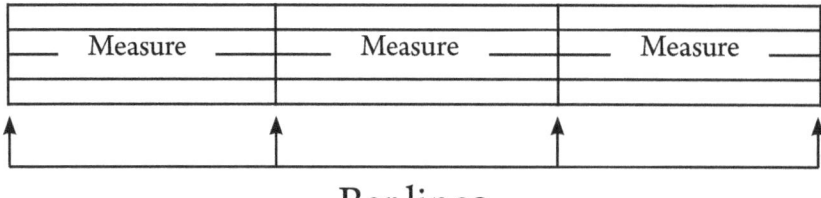

Beats are grouped together in measures. A measure may contain two, three, four or more beats.

Time Signatures

Two numbers are placed at the beginning of a piece of music. These two numbers are called the time signature.

The top number indicates the number of beats in each measure. The bottom number tells us which note gets the beat.

 four beats in each measure

the quarter note gets one beat

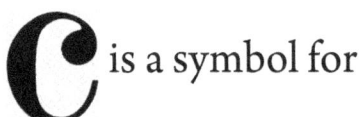 is a symbol for  time, which is also called common time.

1. Number the beats in each measure.

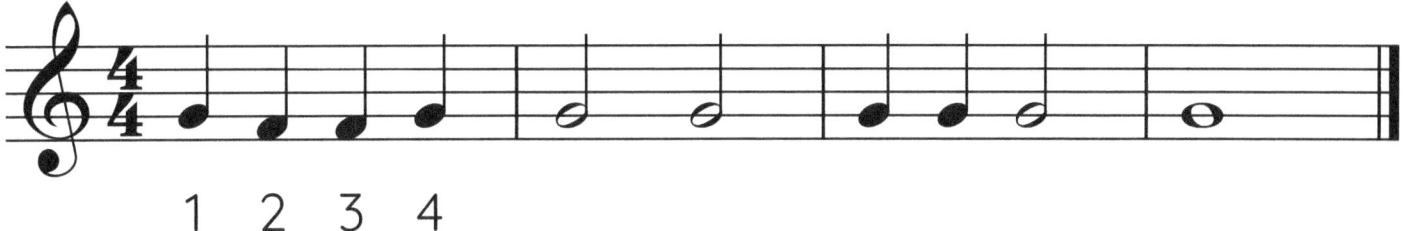

1   2   3   4

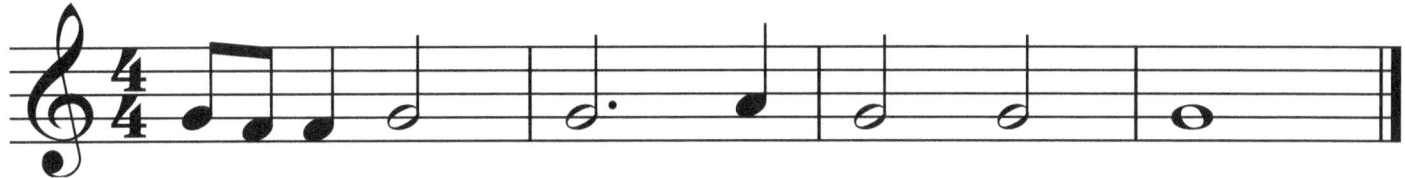

3/4 three beats in each measure

the quarter note gets one beat

---

2. Number the beats in each measure.

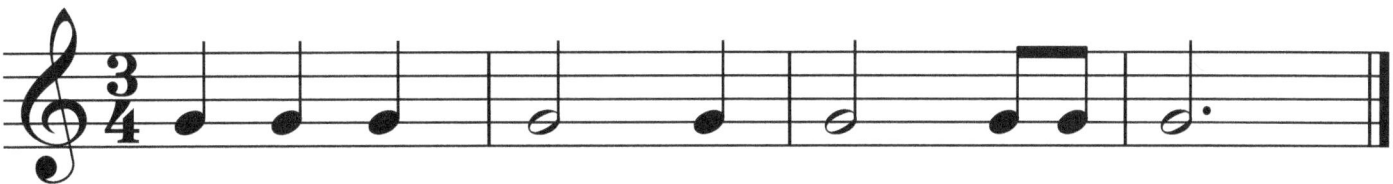

2 two beats in each measure

4 the quarter note gets one beat

3. Number the beats in each measure.

4. Number the beats in each measure. Put the time signature at the beginning of each staff.

5. Divide these staves into measures by adding bar lines.

6. Add one note to complete each measure.

7. Add one rest to complete each measure.

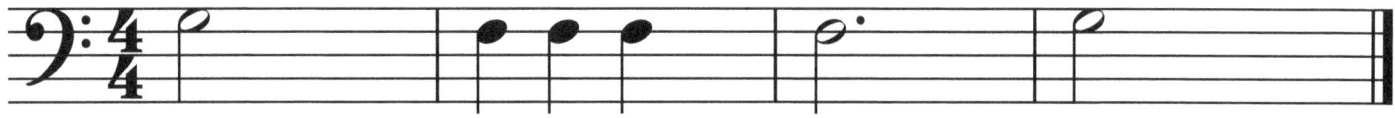

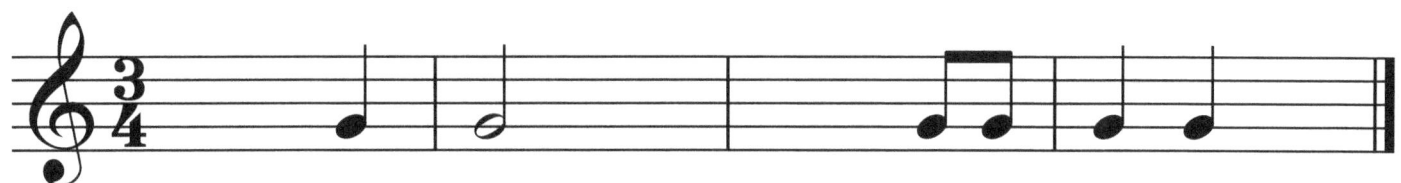

8. Add a time signature at the beginning of each line.

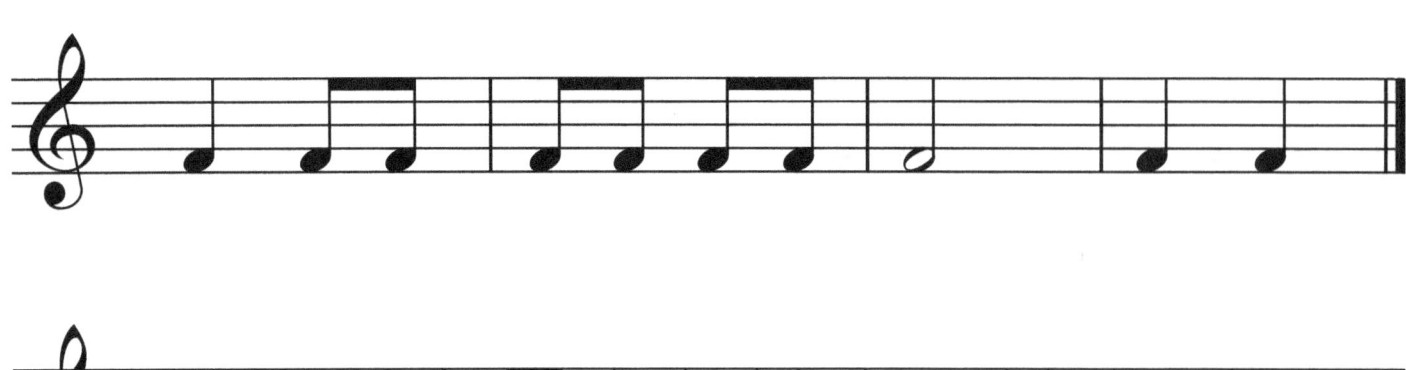

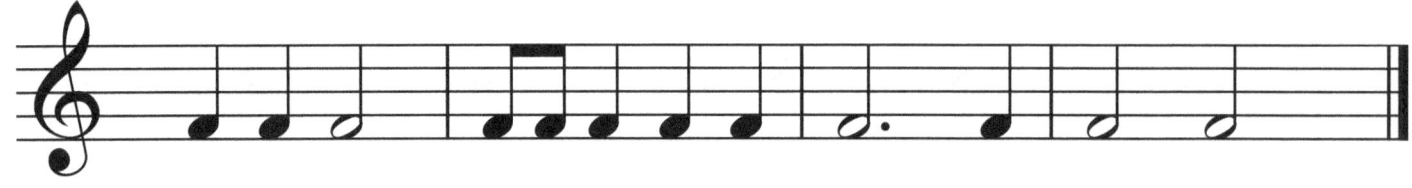

9. Add bar lines according to the time signatures.

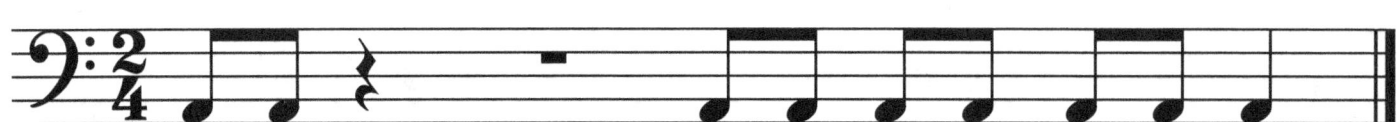

Robert Schumann
(1810-1856)

Robert Schumann was born in Zwickau, a town in southeastern Germany. His father was a bookseller. At a young age, Schumann fell in love with poetry and storytelling. This helped him to develop a strong musical imagination.

Schumann studied law at university, but he devoted his energies to music. He wanted to become a concert pianist, but an injury to his right hand ended this dream. Instead he turned to composing music and writing about it.

Schumann was a poetic composer. His best pieces capture a moment of intense thought or feeling...the way a good poem does. He was also the first great music critic. His reviews of the new music of his day are still worth reading. Schumann's wife, Clara Wieck, one of the greatest pianists of the 19th century, was also an outstanding composer.

The Grand Staff Review

1. Name these notes by writing the letters. Draw lines connecting the notes to the keyboard.

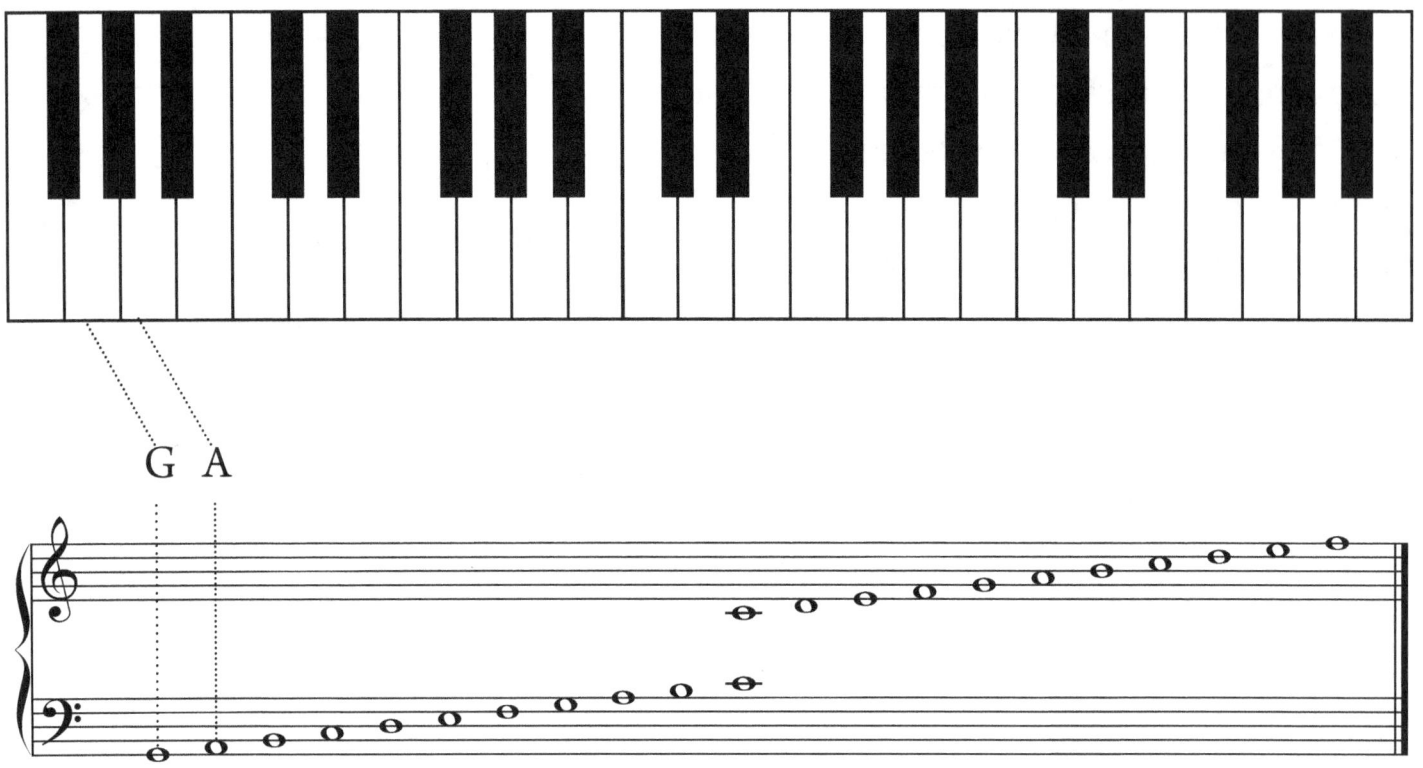

2. Write the correct note above each letter name.

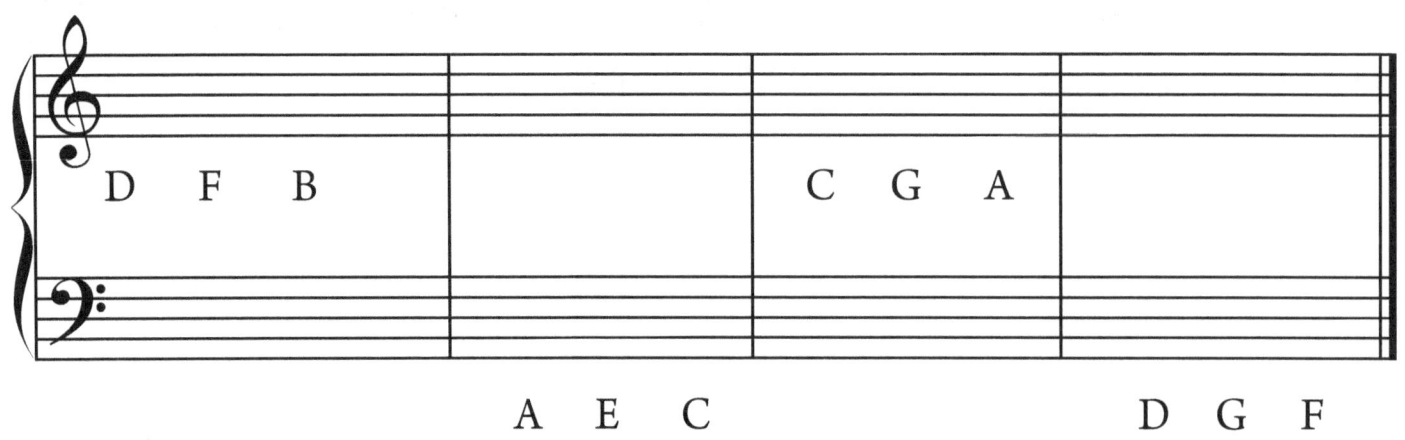

3. Match the notes with the shaded keys.

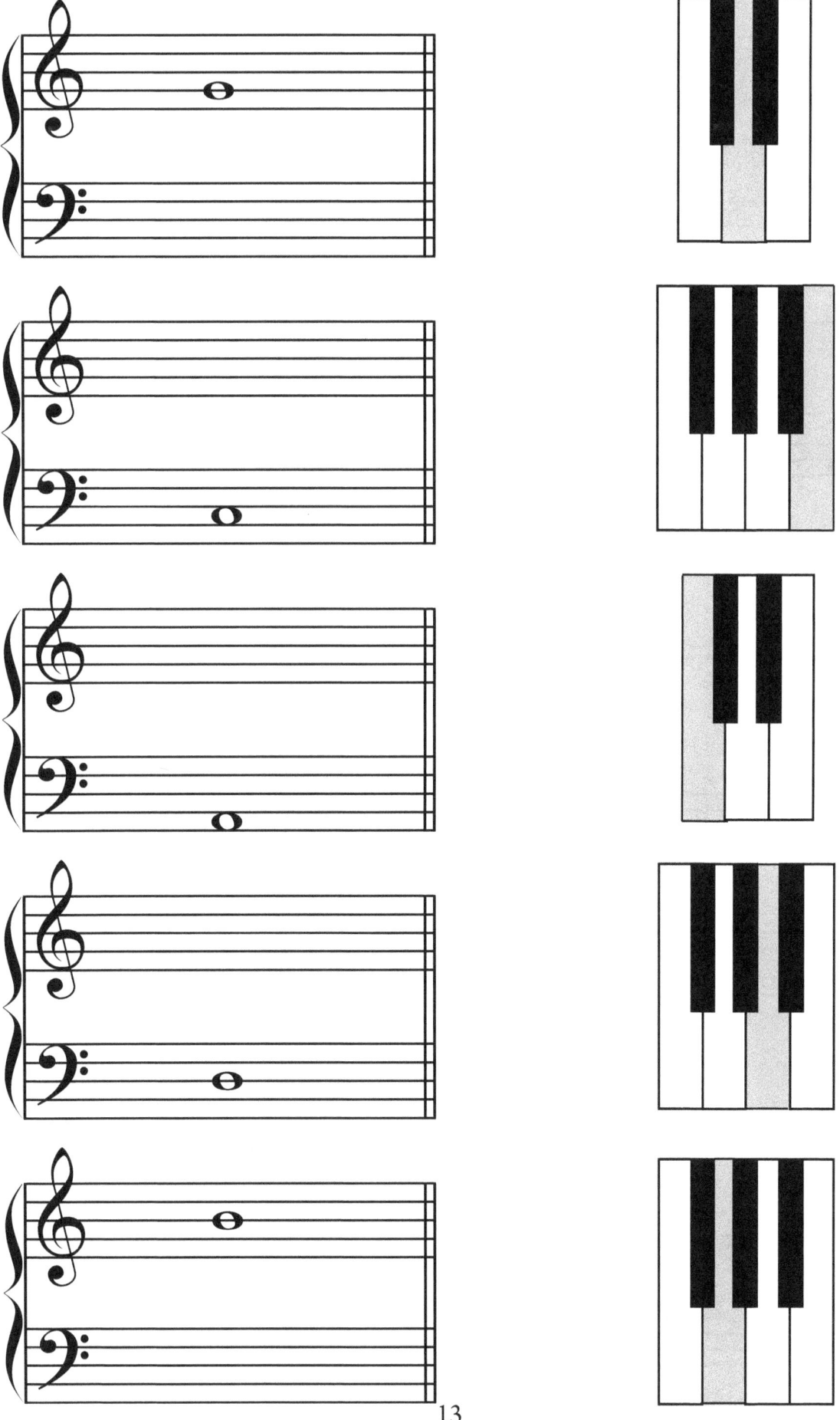

SPELLING FUN

1. Name these notes. They spell words.

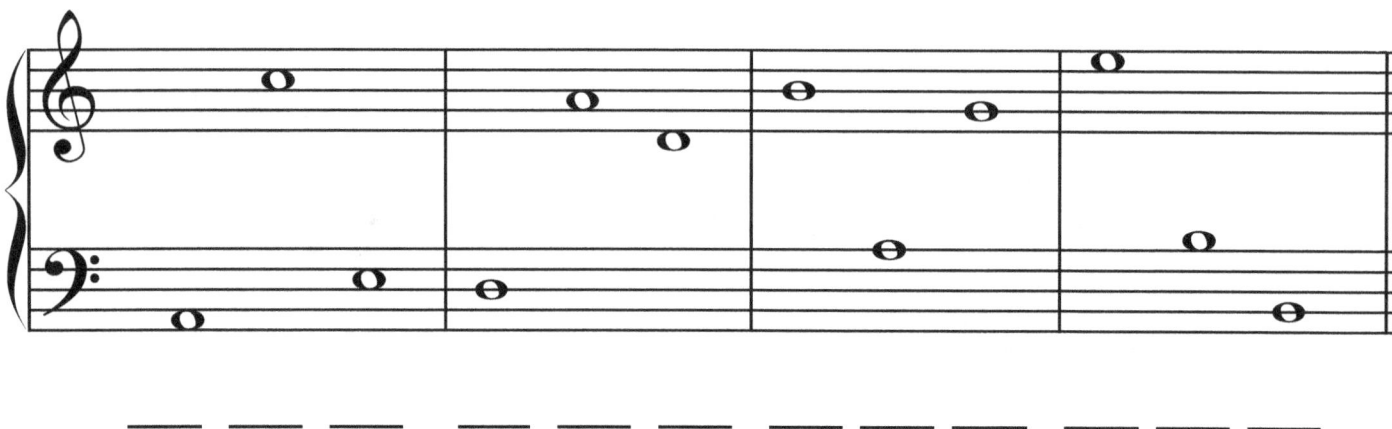

_ _ _ _   _ _ _ _

2. Spell these words using notes on the grand staff.

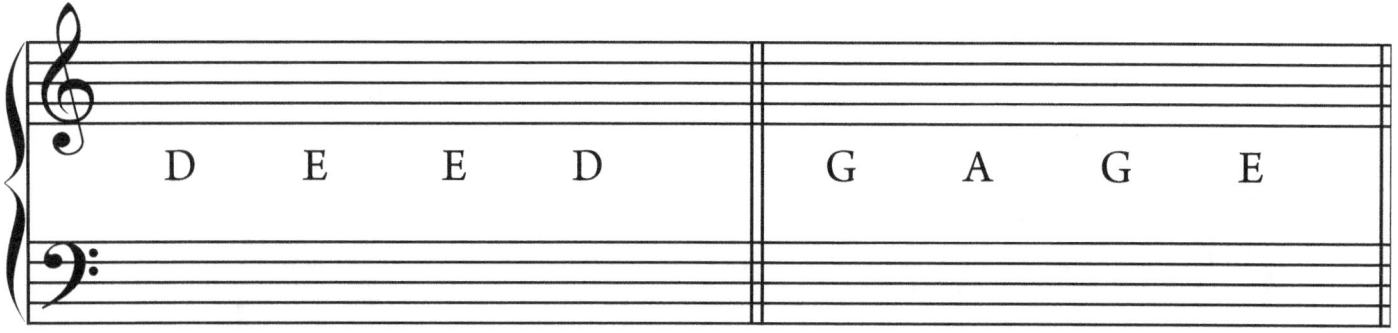

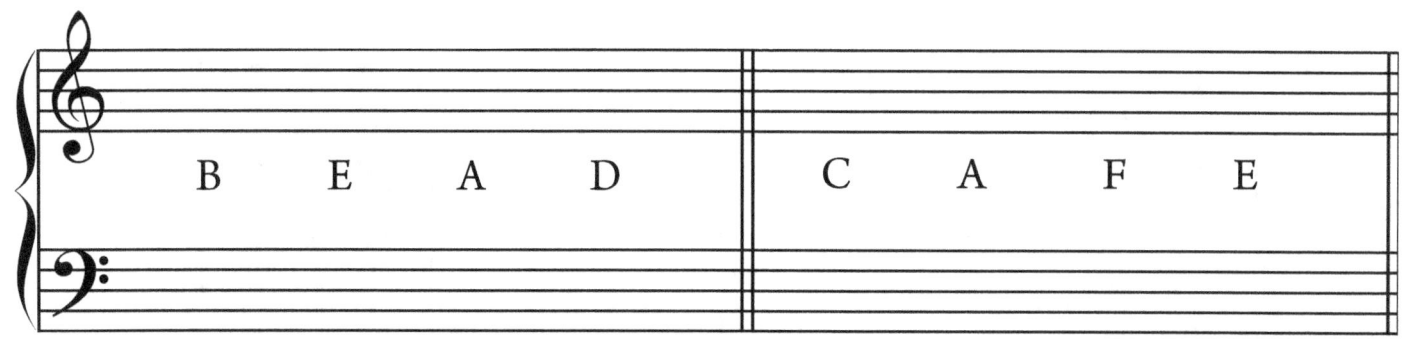

Note Stems

Most notes have stems. Sometimes a note stem goes up, and sometimes it goes down.

Here are the three rules for placing note stems.

1. Notes above the middle line have stems going down.

2. Notes below the middle line have stems going up.

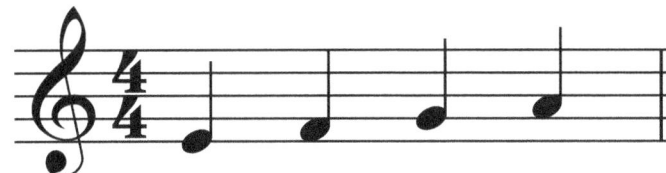

3. Notes on the middle line have stems that go either up or down.

1. Add stems to these notes.

2. Correct any note stems that are wrong.

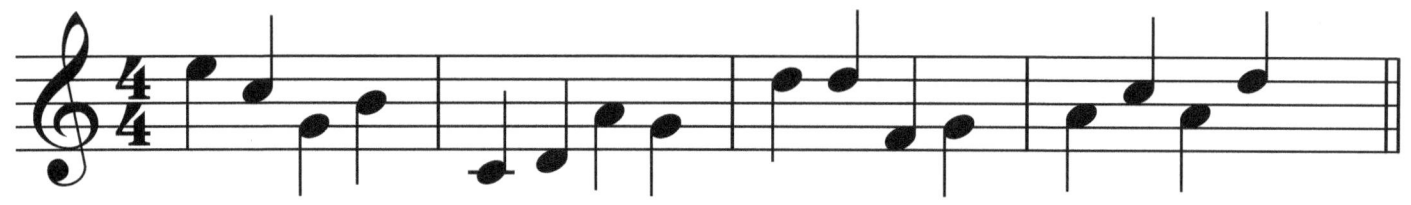

Musical Terms

Terms referring to sound

pianissimo	*pp*	very soft
piano	*p*	soft
mezzo piano	*mp*	moderately soft
mezzo forte	*mf*	moderately loud
forte	*f*	loud
fortissimo	*ff*	very loud

Terms referring to tempo or speed

largo	very slow and broad
andante	moderately slow; at a walking pace
moderato	at a moderate tempo
allegro	fast

Review Quiz 1

1. Divide each staff into meaures by adding bar lines.

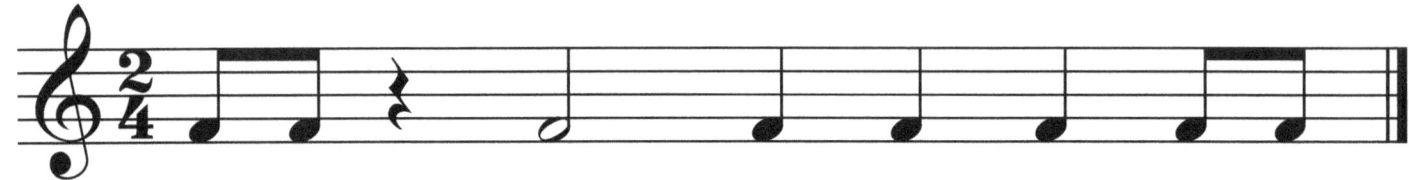

2. Add a time signature to each staff.

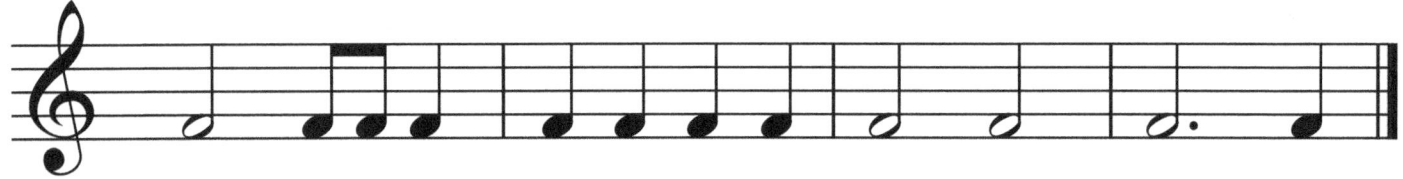

3. Add one note to complete each measure.

4. Write these notes on both the treble and bass clefs on the grand staff.

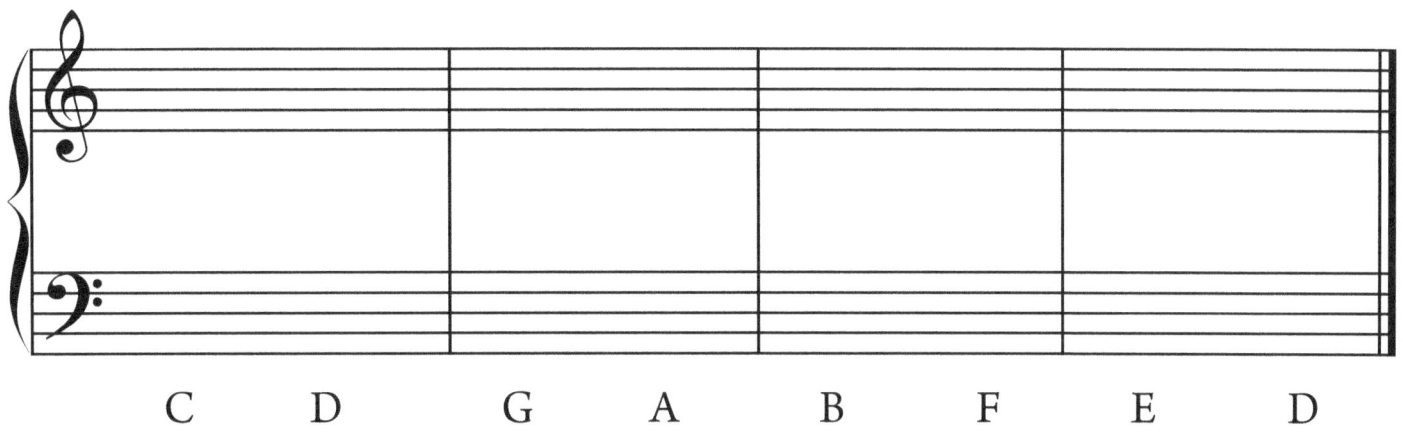

5. Write the sign and meaning of the following Italian terms.

	Sign	Meaning
forte	_____	_____
piano	_____	_____
mezzo forte	_____	_____
fortissimo	_____	_____
pianissimo	_____	_____
mezzo piano	_____	_____

6. Add stems to the following notes.

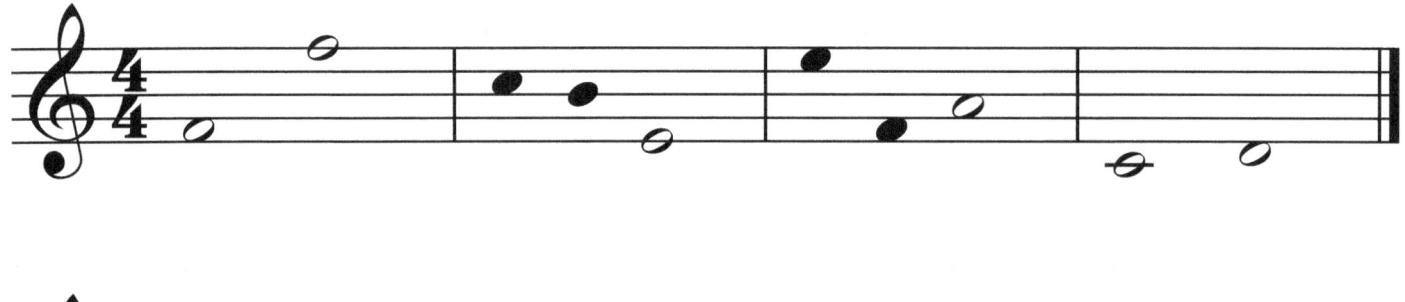

Johannes Brahms
(1833-1897)

Johannes Brahms was born in Hamburg, Germany. As a child, he learned the piano, violin, cello, and horn. In his teens, he was already giving piano recitals, and his piano teacher encouraged him to compose.

Brahms had great respect and love for the music of earlier composers. In his youth, he spent many hours studying old scores. Brahms composed variations on melodies by Handel and Haydn.

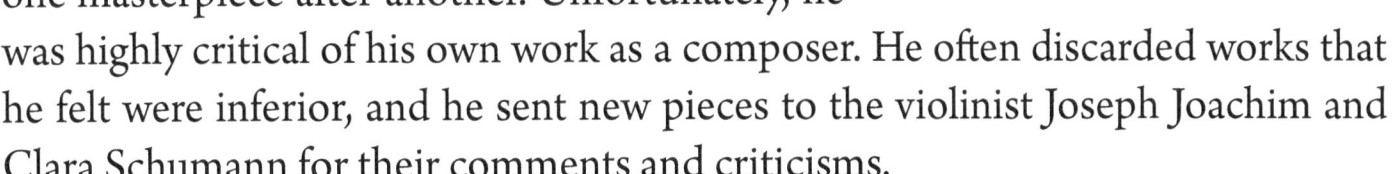

Schumann predicted that the young Brahms would be the next great composer. Robert and Clara Schumann became close, lifetime friends. Brahms settled in Vienna, where he turned out one masterpiece after another. Unfortunately, he was highly critical of his own work as a composer. He often discarded works that he felt were inferior, and he sent new pieces to the violinist Joseph Joachim and Clara Schumann for their comments and criticisms.

Half Steps and Whole Steps

The piano keyboard is made up of half steps.

A half step is the distance from one key to the very next key, black or white.

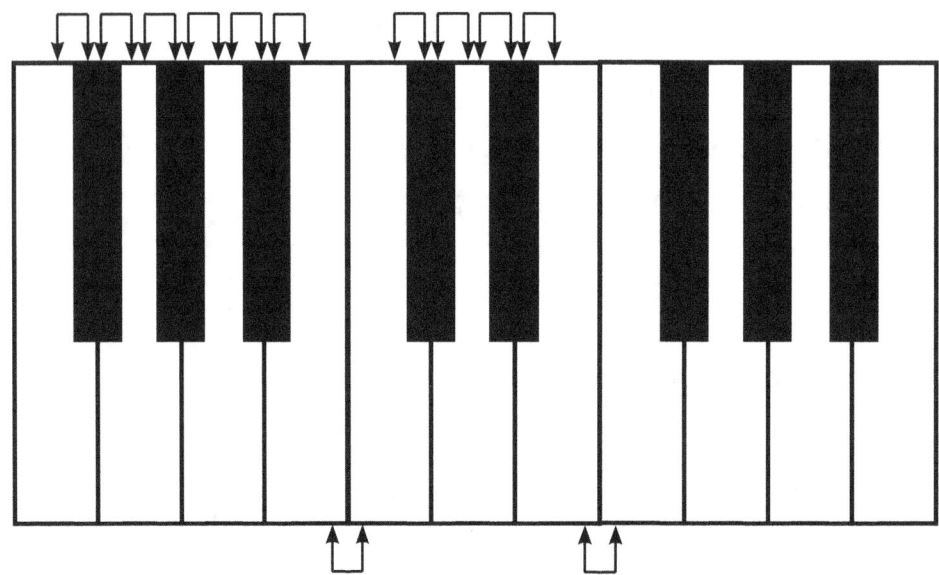

In other words, a half step is the shortest distance between notes on the piano keyboard.

A whole step is made up of two half steps.

On the piano keyboard a whole step is the distance between two keys with one key in between. The key in the middle can be either black or white.

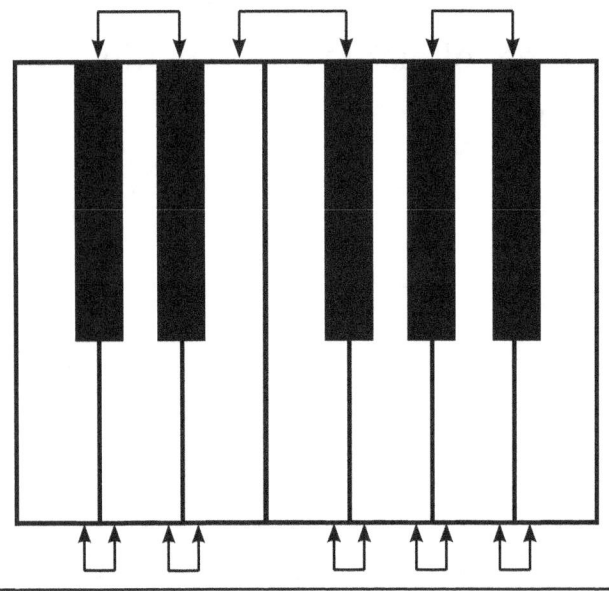

In other words a whole step can be:
- from a white key to a white key
- from a black key to a black key
- from a white key to a black key
- from a black key to a white key
- but one key must always be skipped.

Sharps

A sharp ♯ raises a note one half step.

A note with a sharp sign is played on the next key to the right... one half step higher.

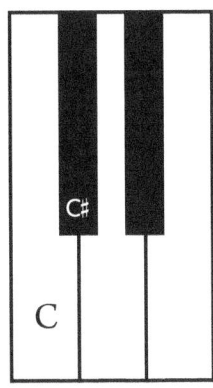 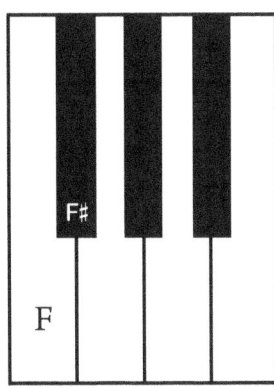

Sharps are usually...but not always...played on black keys.

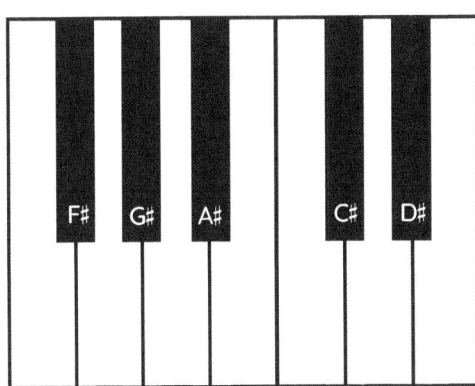 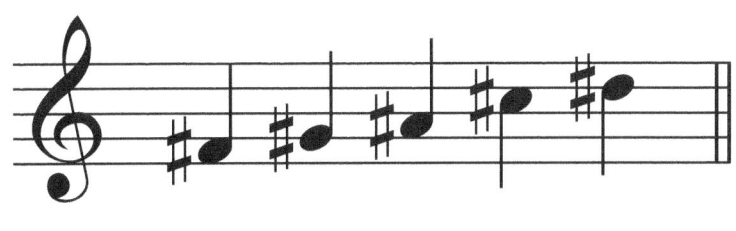

Sharps are written in front of a note. The middle part of the sign is on the same line or space as the note.

If a note is on a line, the middle of the sharp is on the same line.

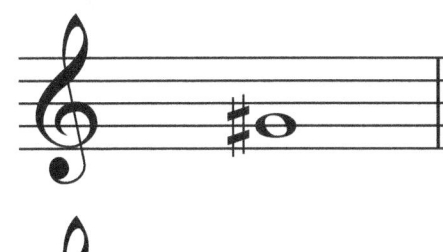

If a note is in a space, the middle of the sharp is in the same space.

1. Practice drawing sharps on lines.

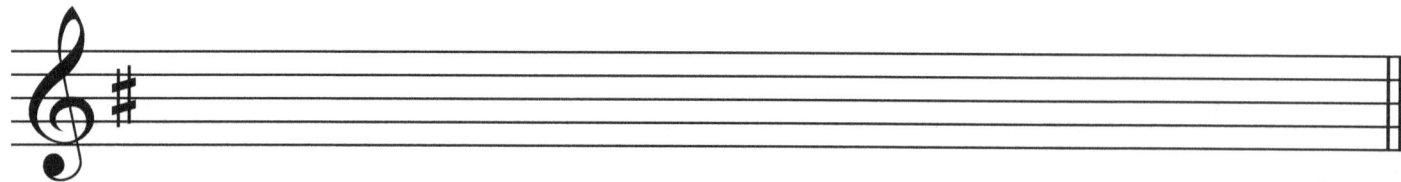

2. Practice drawing sharps in spaces.

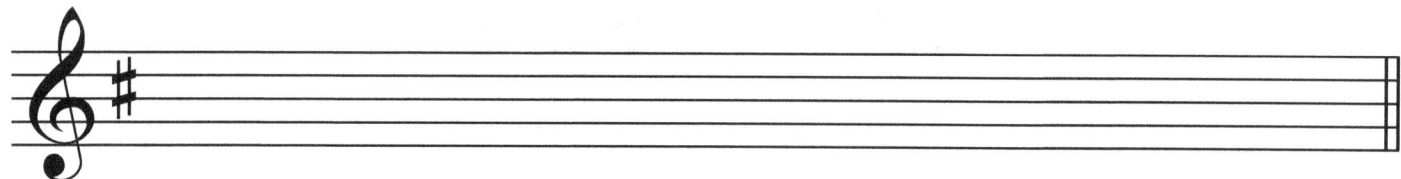

3. Name each note and color in the key on the keyboard.

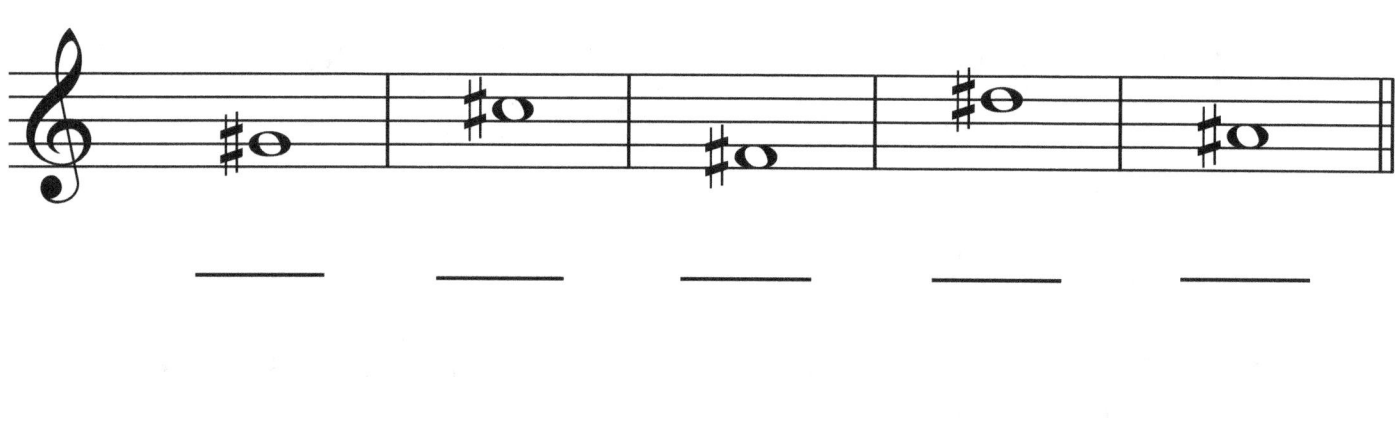

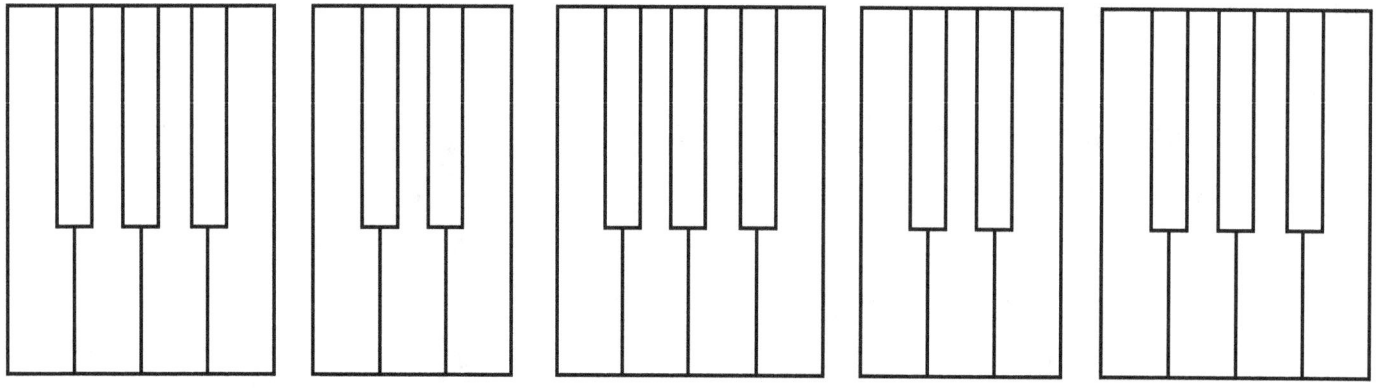

4. Put sharp signs in front of the second note in each measure.
   Name all the notes, then play them.

5. Write these notes using half notes.

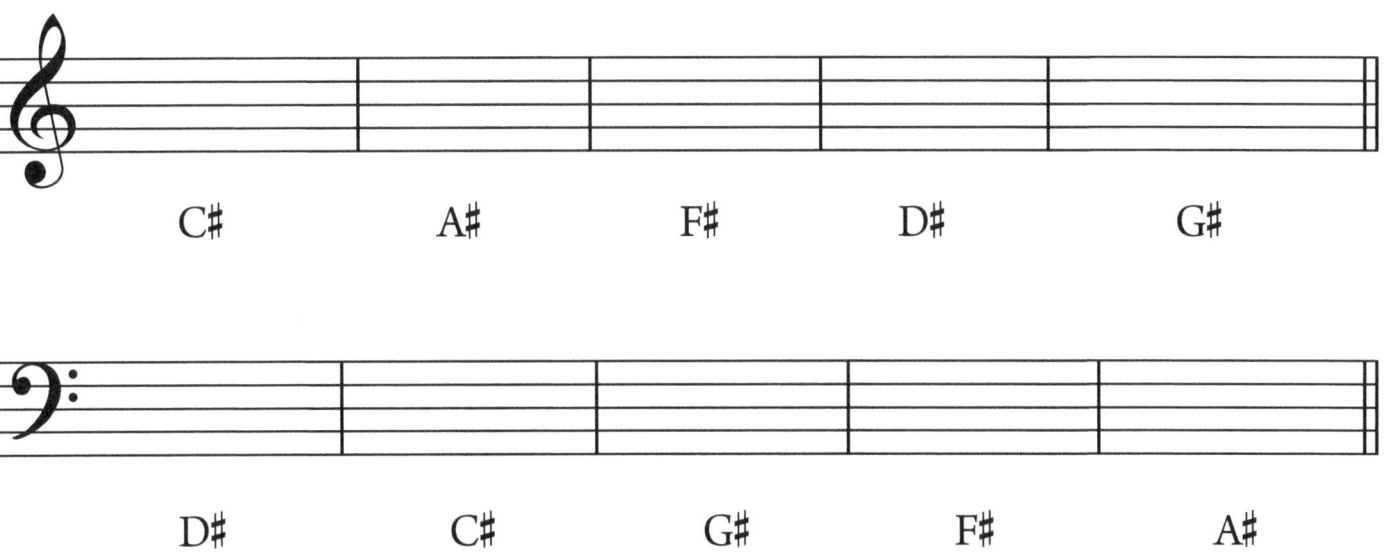

Flats

A flat ♭ lowers a note one half step.

A note with a flat sign is played on the next key to the left... one half step lower.

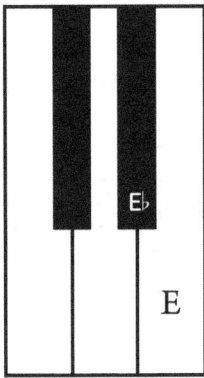 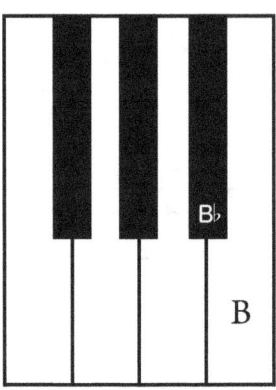

Flats are usually...but not always...played on black keys.

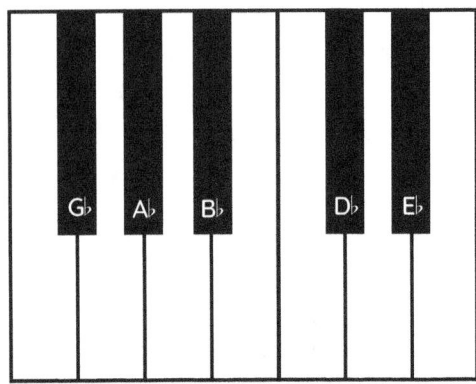 

Flats are written in front of a note. The middle part of the loop is on the same line or space as the note.

If a note is on a line, the middle of the loop is on the same line.

If a note is in a space, the middle of the loop is in the same space.

1. Practice drawing flats on lines.

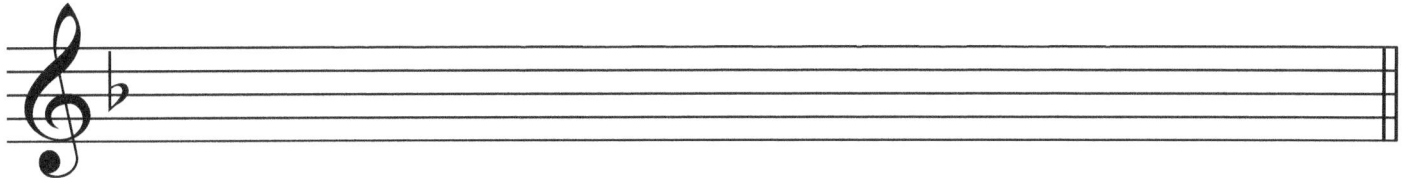

2. Practice drawing flats in spaces.

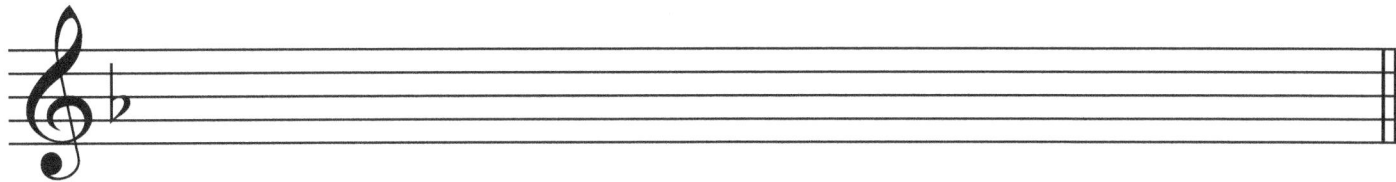

3. Name each note and color in the key on the keyboard.

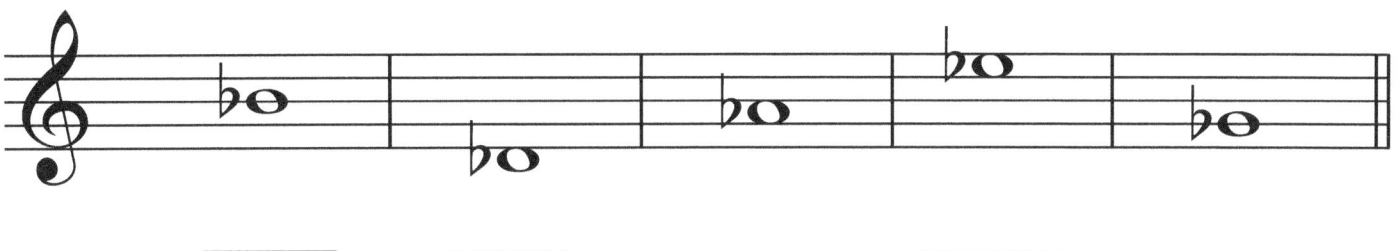

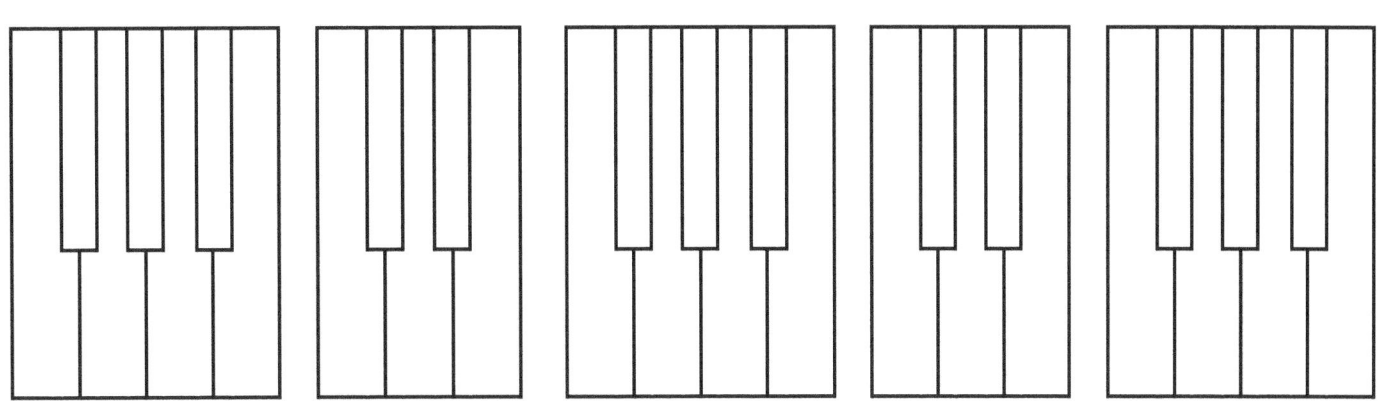

4. Put flat signs in front of the second note in each measure.
   Name all the notes, then play them.

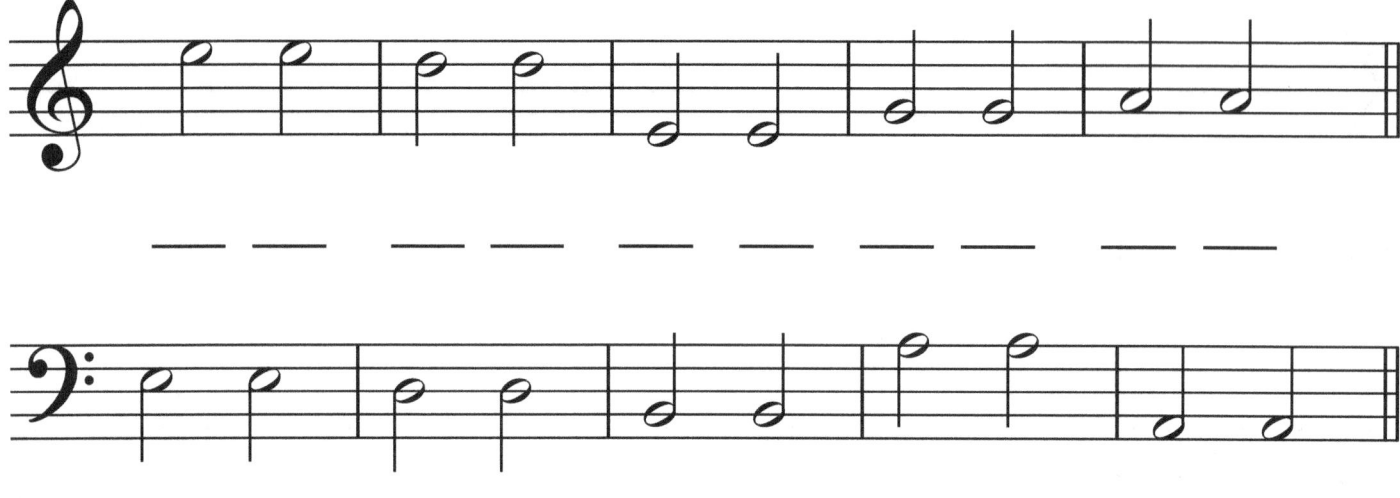

5. Write these notes using quarter notes.

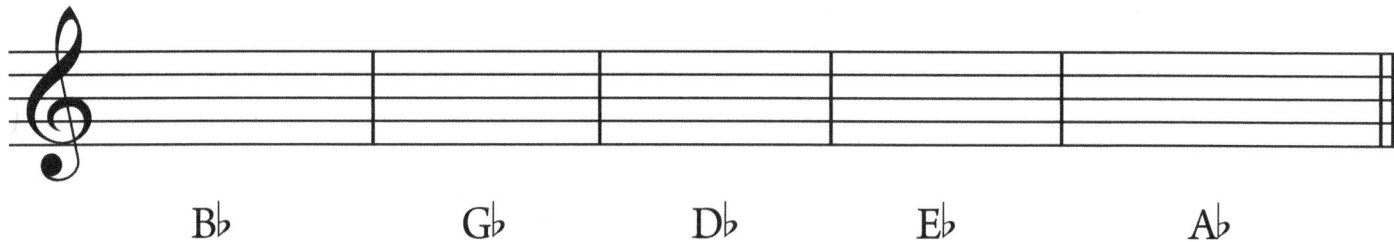

6. Name these notes. Write the number of beats that each note receives.

name: ___ ___ ___ ___ ___ ___ ___ ___

beats: ___ ___ ___ ___ ___ ___ ___ ___

7. Write these notes in the treble clef and the bass clef, using half notes.

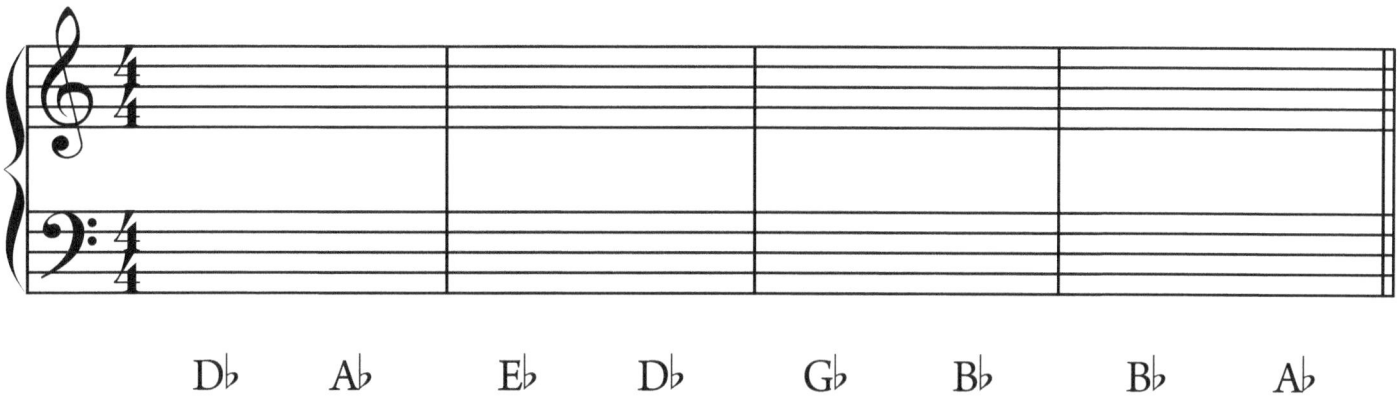

8. Write these notes in the treble clef and the bass clef, using quarter notes.

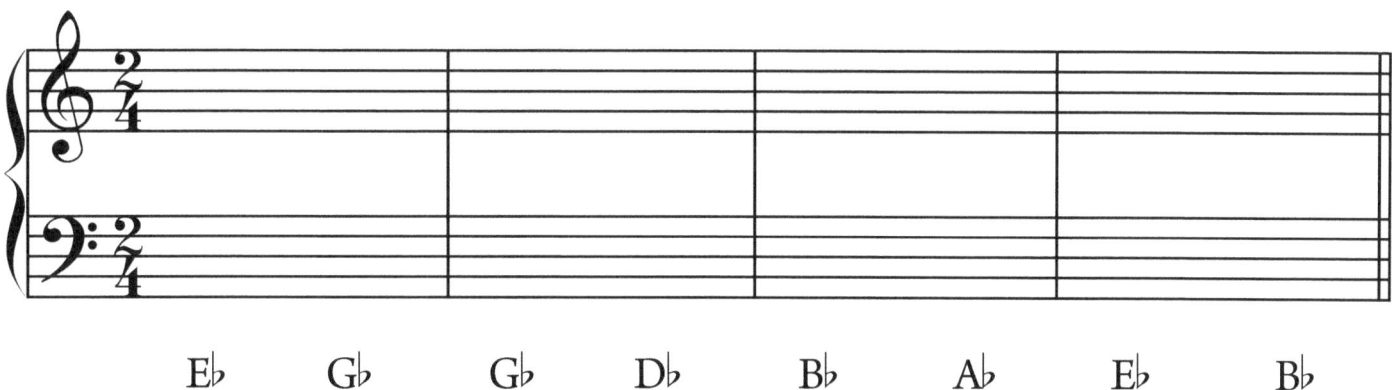

MUSICAL WORD SEARCH

Find words from the list below in this puzzle

```
W Q F S I G N A T U R E C U T
S F L A T T M E A S U R E P I
T Y J R N H J W R D H C U G M
E R A I S E E R E S T B A Y E
M W H O L E S T E P A A S E
P M G C D O W N Y A I R H T T
E J D N D D V L D Y I L B A K
X V S H A R P Z M A Z I E F F
T F Q A B L O W E R W N A F P
T E H A L F S T E P D E T V F
```

staff	sharp
flat	stem
up	down
time	signature
raise	measure
bar line	beat
rest	whole step
half step	lower

Sharps and Flats on White Keys

Not all sharps and flats are played on black keys.

A sharp raises a note one half step.

There are two sharps on white keys: E# and B#

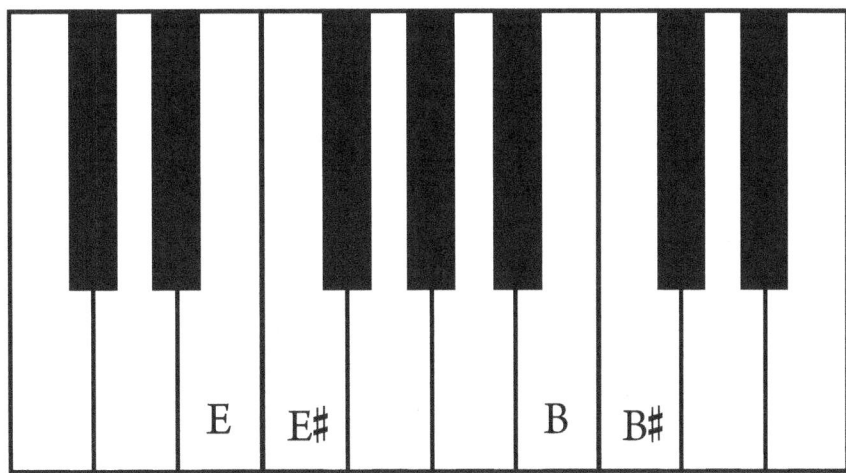

A flat lowers a note one half step.

There are two flats on white keys: F♭ and C♭

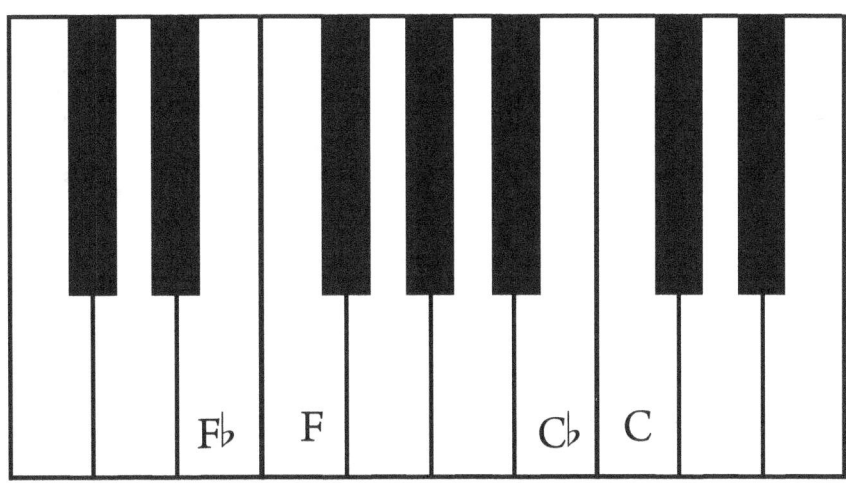

1. Name these notes. Draw lines conecting them to the keys on the keyboard.

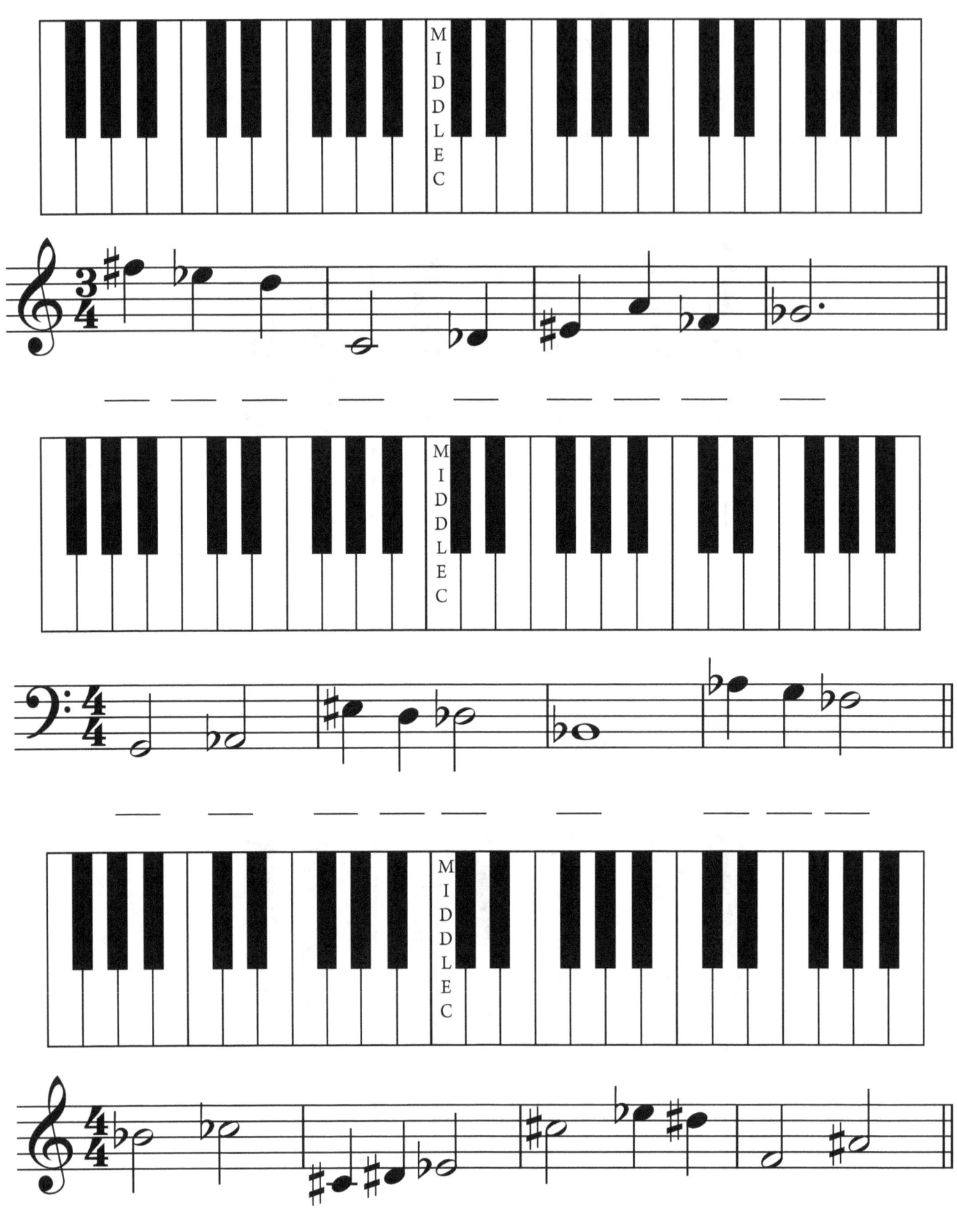

The Natural Sign

A natural ♮ cancels a sharp or flat.

Naturals are written in front of the note. The middle of the natural sign is on the same line or space as the note.

If a note is on a line, the middle of the natural sign is on the same line.

If a note is in a space, the middle of the natural sign is in the same space.

A natural lowers a sharp one half step.

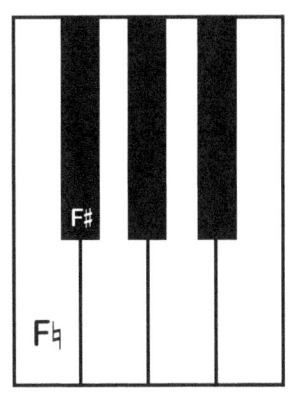

A natural raises a flat one half step.

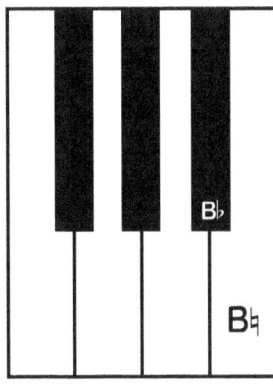

1. Practice drawing natural signs on lines.

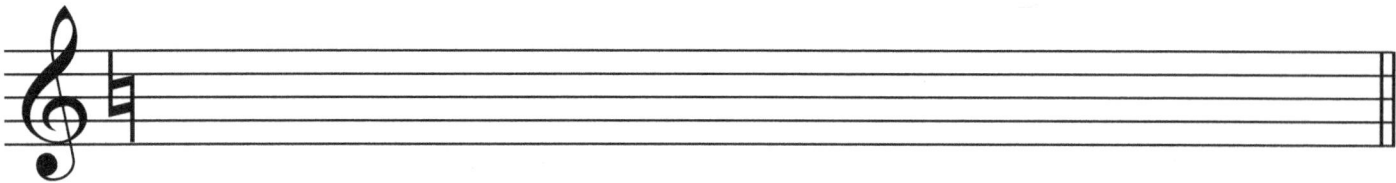

2. Practice drawing natural signs in spaces.

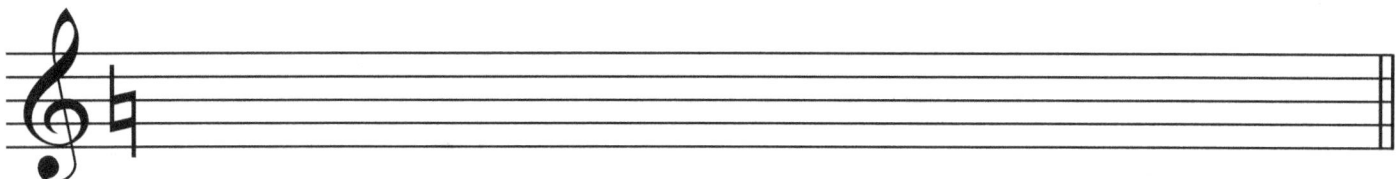

3. Put natural signs in front of the second note in each measure. Name the notes, then play them.

4. Put natural signs in front of the second note in each measure. Name the notes, then play them.

Accidentals

Sharps, flats and naturals are called accidentals. ♯ ♭ ♮

- An accidental changes the pitch of a note.
- An accidental placed in front of a note alters the note until the next bar line.
- A bar line cancels all accidentals in the previous measure.
- An accidental alters only the note that it is in front of. If middle C has a sharp, only middle C is altered, not any other Cs on other lines or spaces.

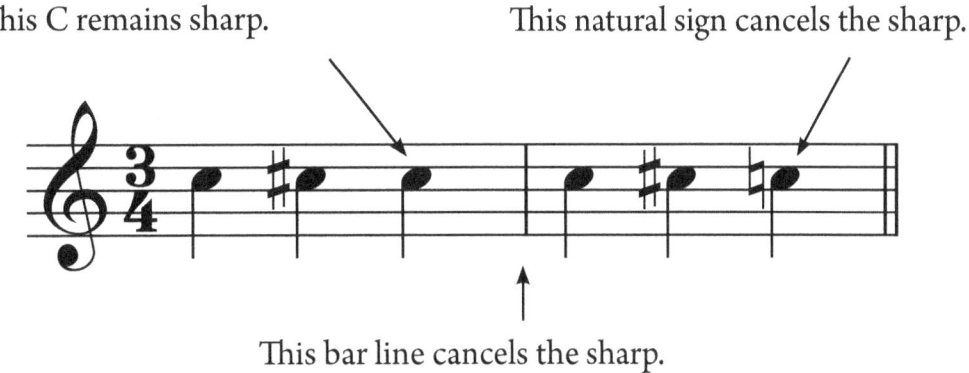

When we use accidentals, many notes can have more than one name.

Look at this example. Even though C♯ and D♭ are two different names, they are the same note. When two notes have different names but sound the same, it is called an enharmonic spelling. C♯ and D♭ are enharmonically the same.

1. Draw lines matching the two notes that are the same but spelled differently.

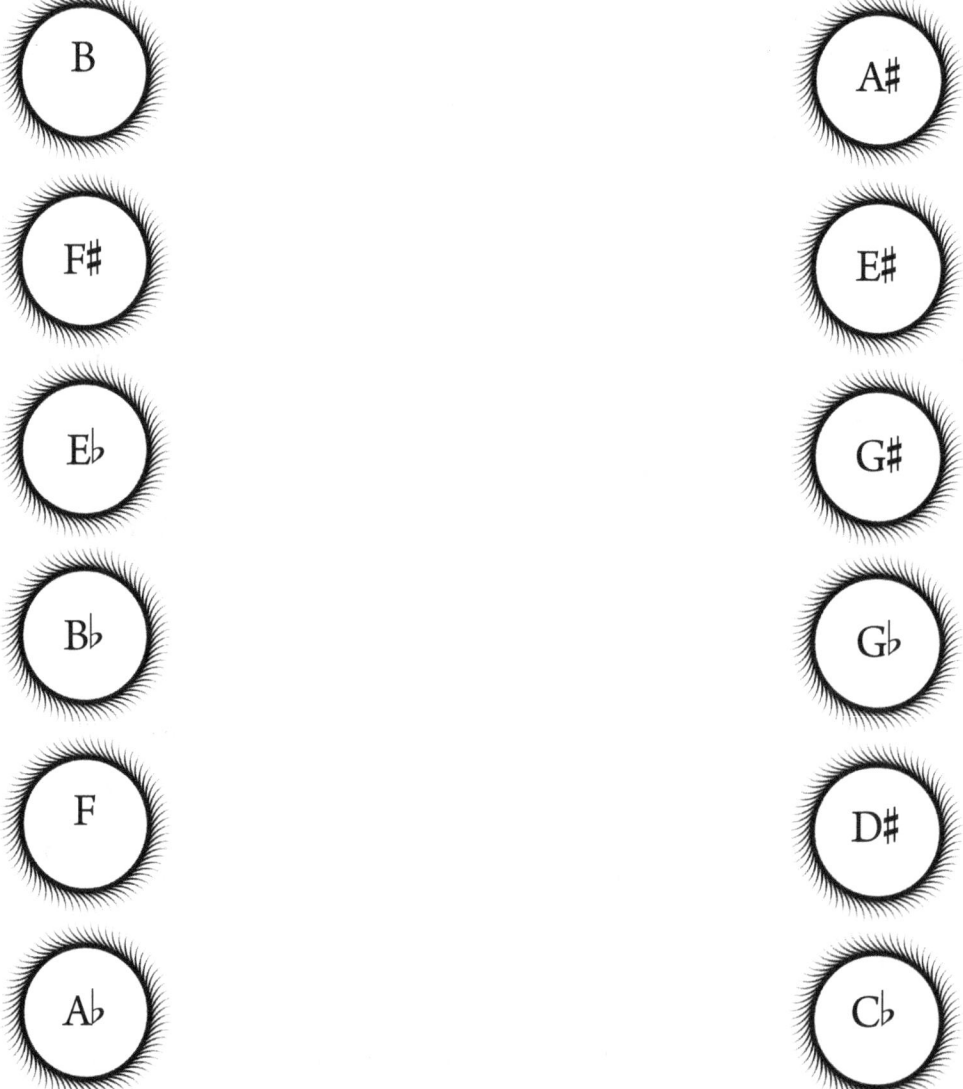

2. Name each note and color in the key on the keyboard.

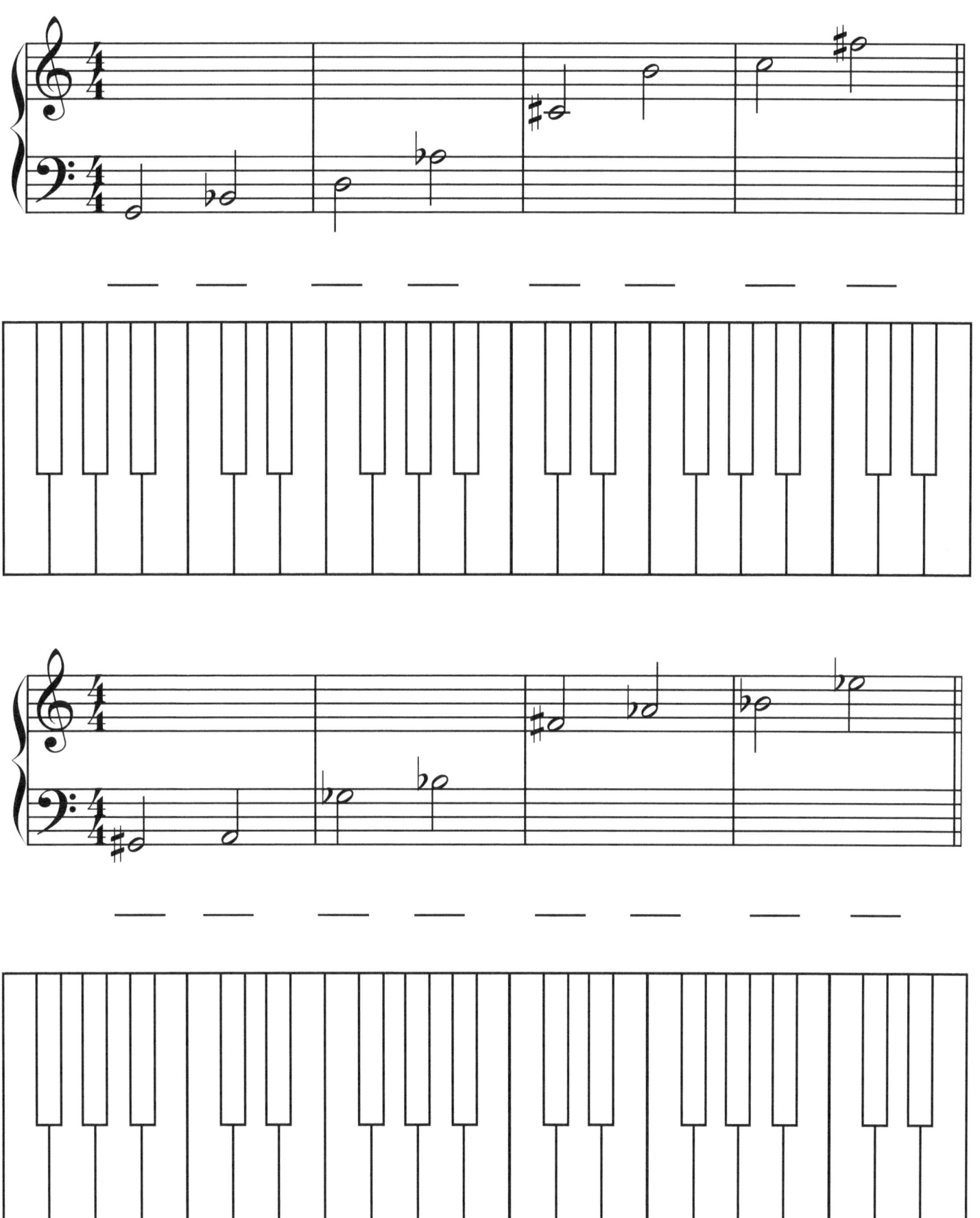

Review the information on whole steps on page 21. The two notes that make up a whole step usually have different letter names. The two letter names are next to each other in the alphabet.

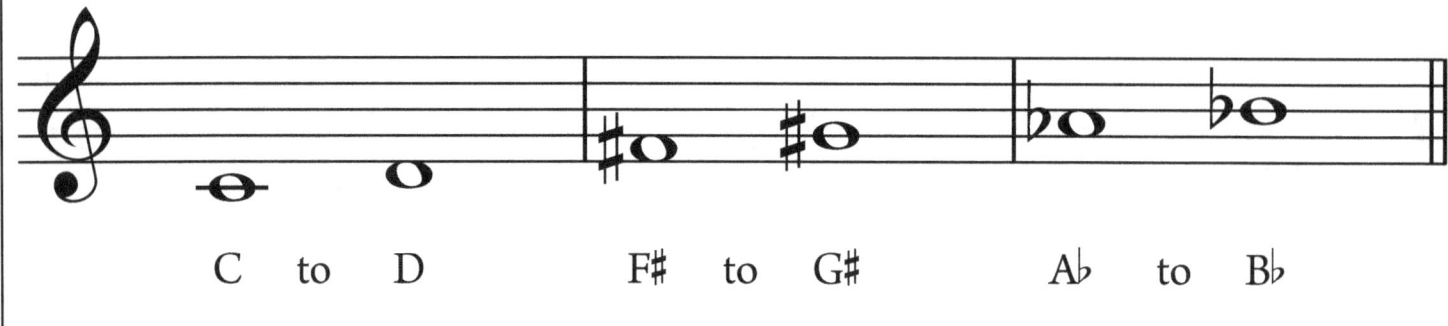

3. Writes notes that are one whole step above the following notes. Name the two notes.

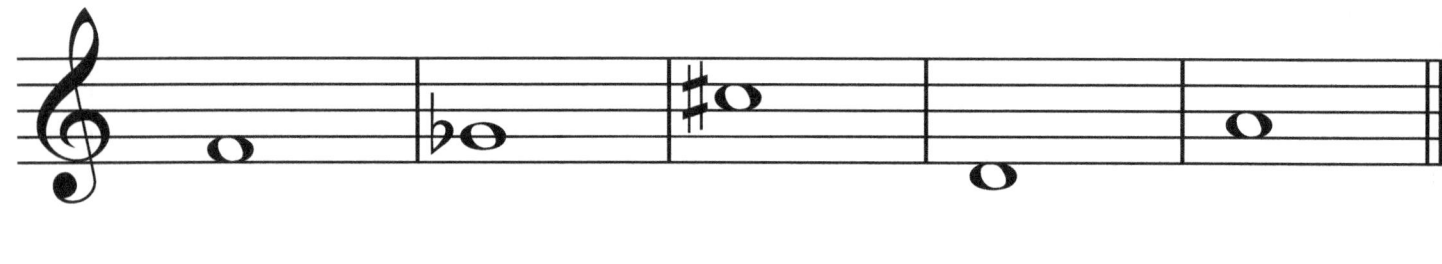

4. Name the following notes. State whether the distance between each is a whole step or a half step.

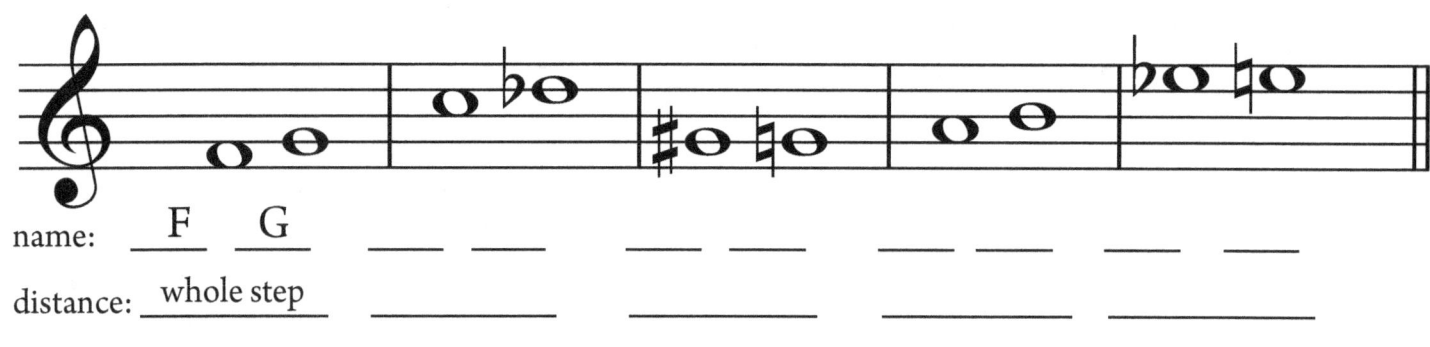

5. Circle the correct answer or answers (there may be more than one).

What is the note that is a whole step above G?

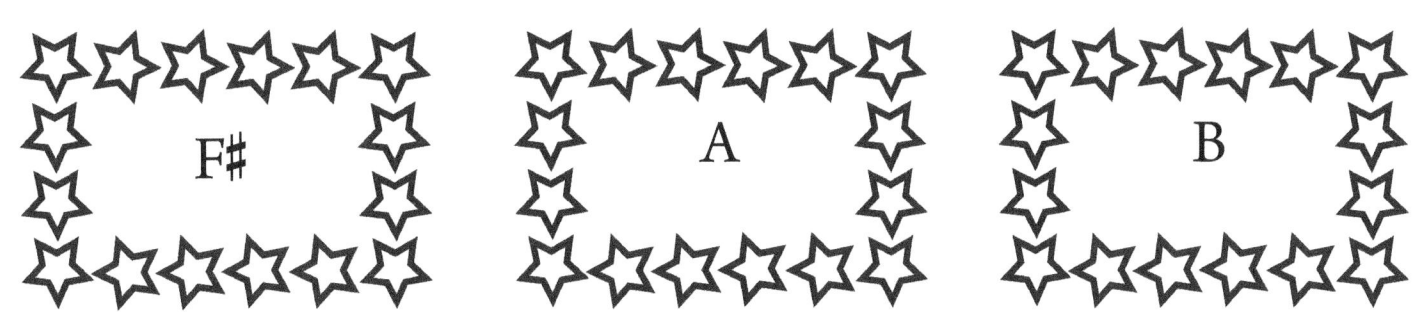

What is the note that is a half step below F?

What is the note that is a half step above C?

What is the note that is a whole step below F?

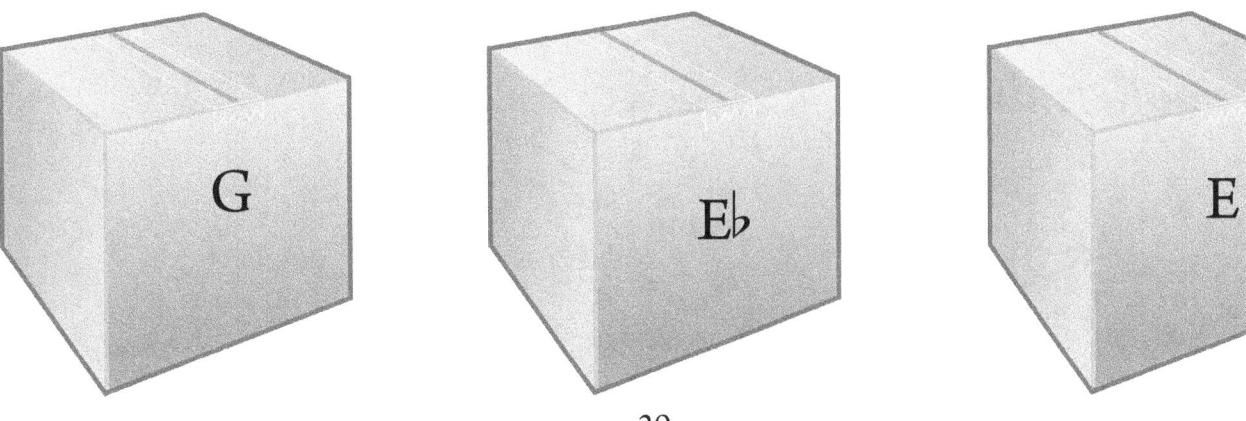

MATCHING QUIZ

Draw lines matching the terms with their meanings.

pp	very slow
mp	loud
largo	fast
p	very soft
andante	moderately loud
ff	soft
allegro	moderately slow; walking pace
f	at a moderate tempo
moderato	very loud
mf	moderately soft

Frédéric Chopin
(1810-1849)

Chopin was born in a small village near Warsaw in Poland. From an early age it was clear that his only real interest in life was music, and his only real interest in music was the piano. Little distracted him from his study of music.

He seemed cut out for a career as a piano virtuoso when he came to Paris in 1831. However, once he was settled in Paris, he rarely appeared in public. Instead, he flourished in the private salons of the wealthy.

Chopin chose to make his living by publishing his music and giving lessons to well-to-do pupils. Most of Chopin's compositions are for piano solo. He also had a long relationship with the French novelist Aurore Dudevant, who wrote under the name George Sand. When this ended, Chopin's already poor health declined rapidly. He died of tuberculosis at age thirty-nine.

Intervals

An interval is the distance between two notes. We can determine the size of an interval by counting the names of the notes of the interval.

C to D in an interval of a 2nd.
There are two letter names from C to D.

$$C - D$$
$$1 - 2$$

D to A in an interval of a 5th.
There are five letter names from D to A.

$$D - E - F - G - A$$
$$1 - 2 - 3 - 4 - 5$$

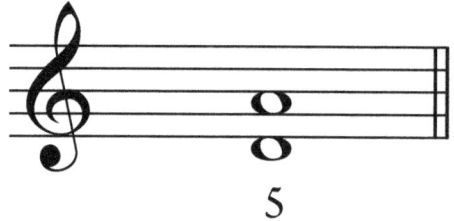

Here are all the intervals up to an octave (8th).

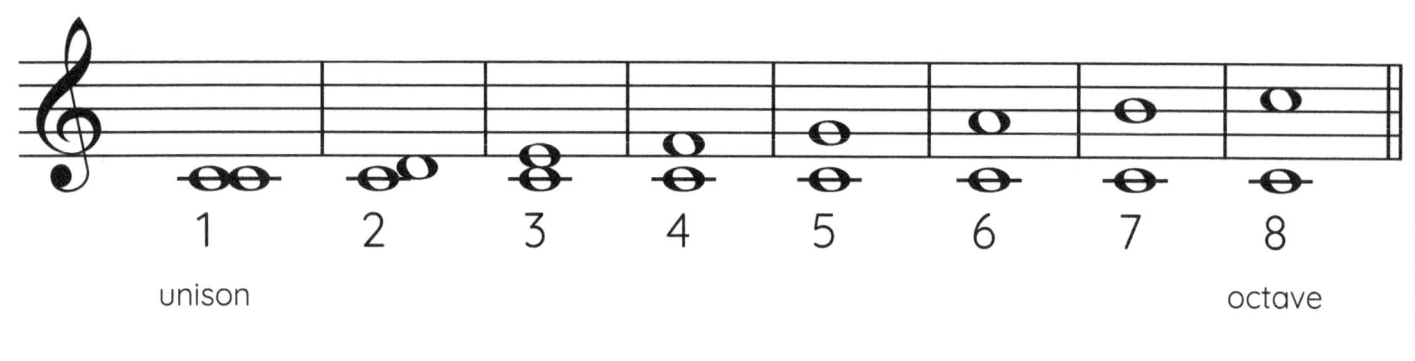

1. Write the number name of the following intervals.

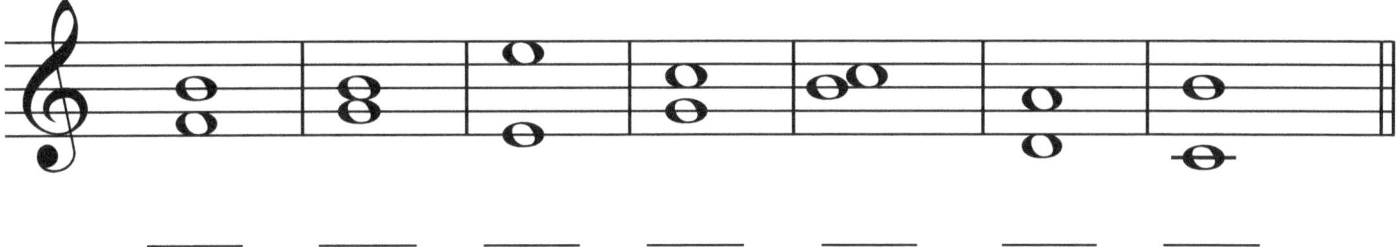

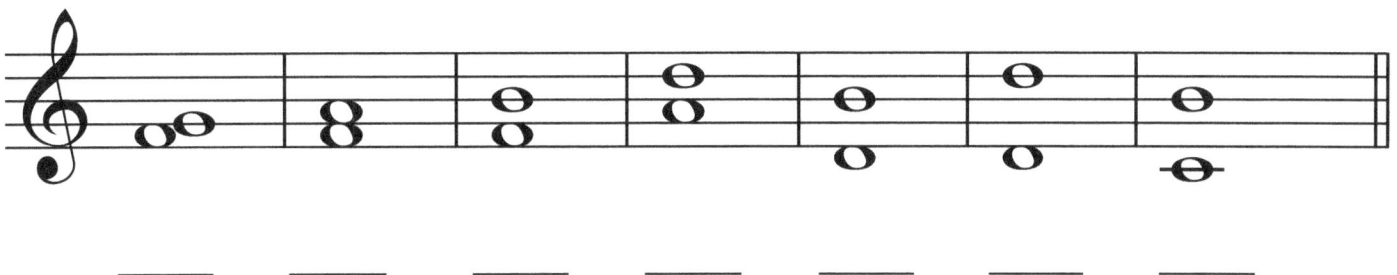

2. **Write these intervals above the given notes.**

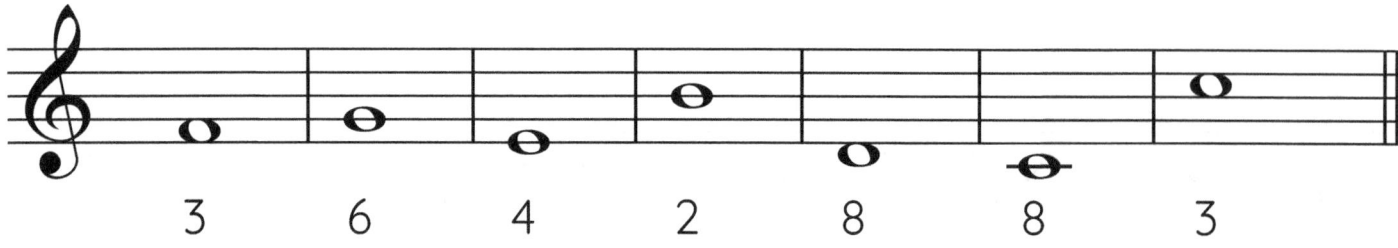

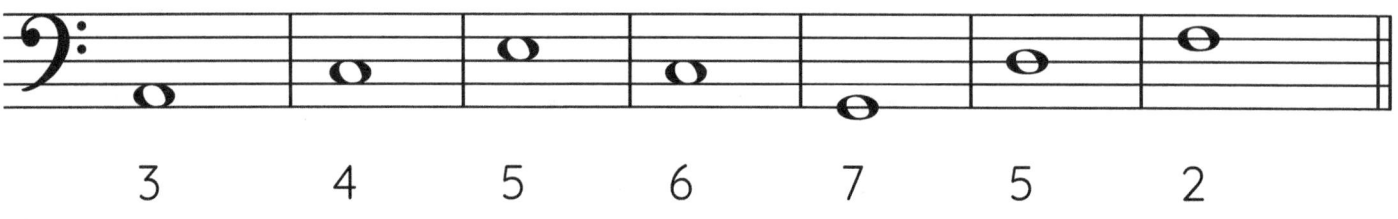

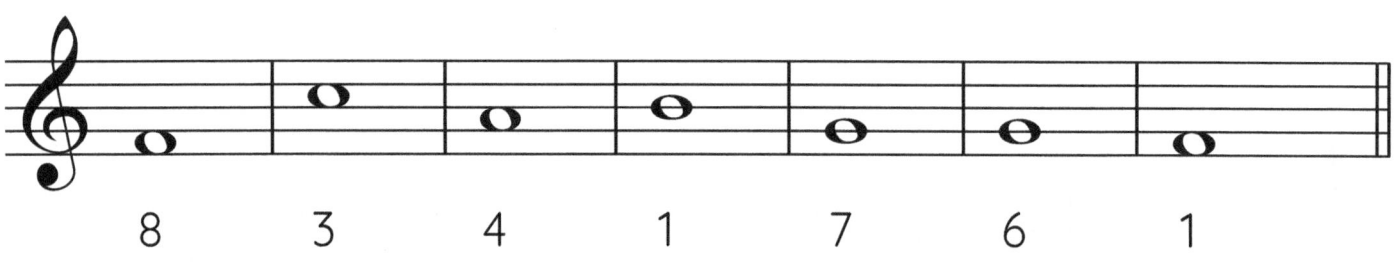

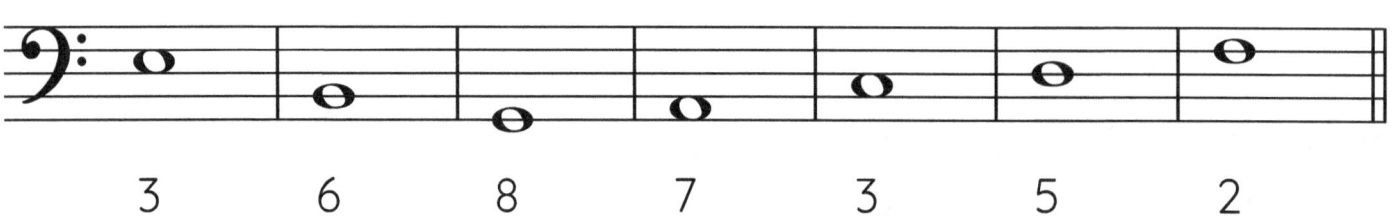

Harmonic and Melodic Intervals

An interval in which the notes are played one after the other (like the notes of a melody) is called a melodic interval.

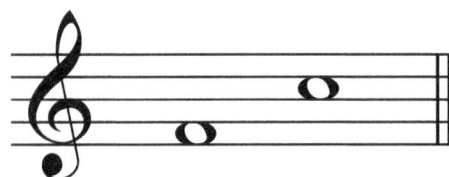

An interval in which the notes are played at the same time (like harmony) is called a harmonic interval.

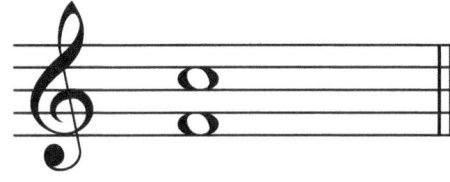

1. Write these melodic intervals above the given notes.

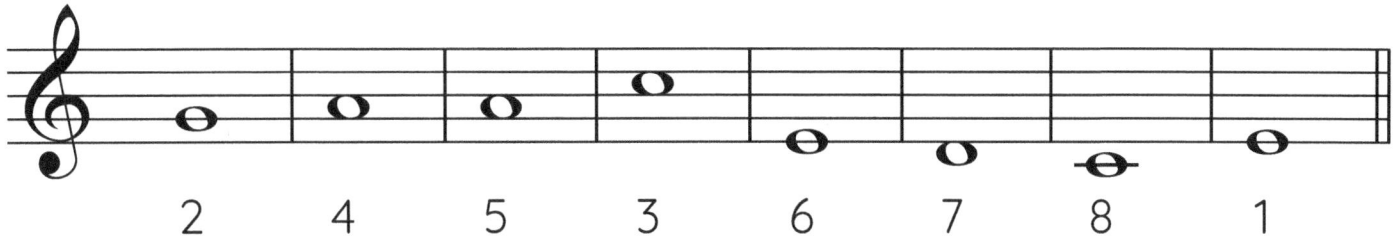

2. Write these harmonic intervals above the given notes.

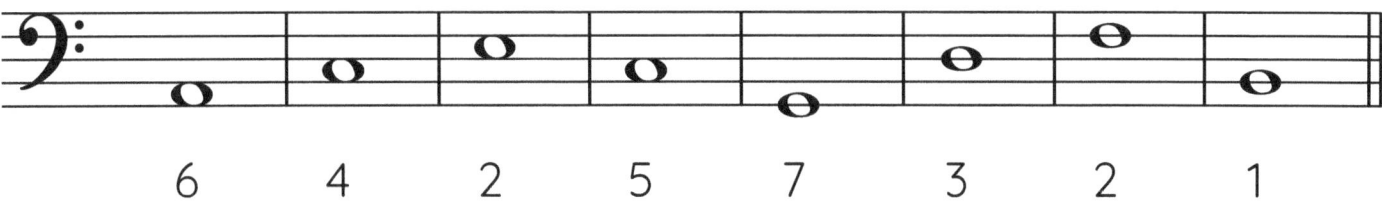

3. Fill in the blanks using the list of words below.

(a) A _____ raises a note by one half step.

(b) A _____ lowers a note by one half step.

(c) The shortest distance between two notes on the keyboard called a _____.

(d) A _____ cancels a sharp or flat.

(e) A natural sign _____ a sharp one half step.

(f) A natural sign _____ a flat one semitone.

(g) An _____ is the distance between two notes.

(h) An interval in which the notes are played one after the other is called a _____ interval.

(i) An interval in which the notes are played at the same time is called a _____ interval.

(j) A _____ is made up of two half steps.

sharp   raises
whole step   natural
flat   half step
melodic   lowers
interval   harmonic

Review Quiz 2

1. Name these notes.

2. Match the Italian terms with their meanings.

    moderato   very slowly

    allegro   at a moderate tempo

    andante   fast

    largo   moderately slow; at a walking pace

3. Rewrite these notes at the same pitch, Then, using an accidental, raise the new note one half step.

10

4. Rewrite these notes at the same pitch, Then, using an accidental, lower the new note one half step.

10

5. Identify these pairs of notes as half steps (HS) or whole steps (WS).

10

6. Write the number name of the following intervals.

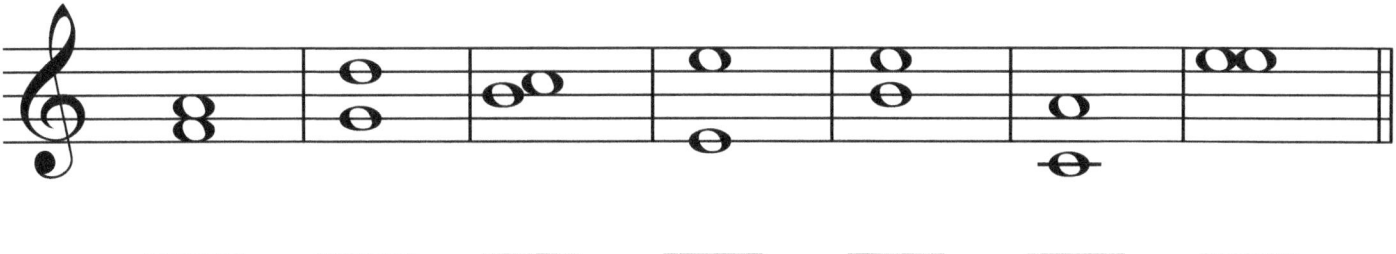

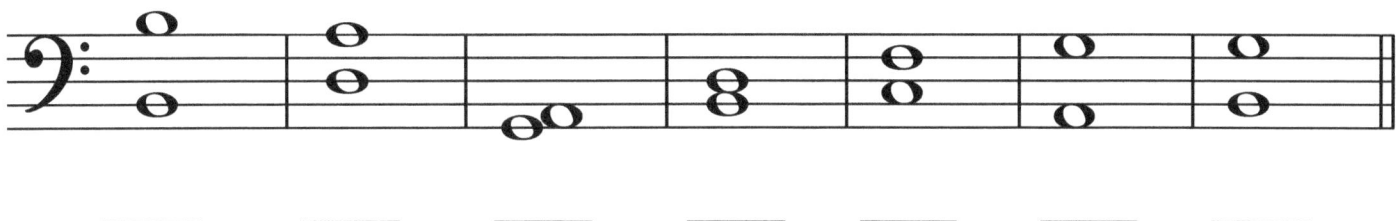

_____
14

7. Write these intervals above the given notes.

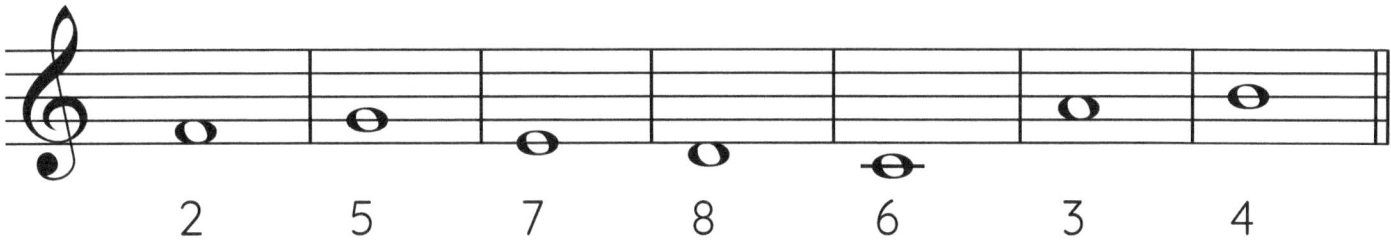

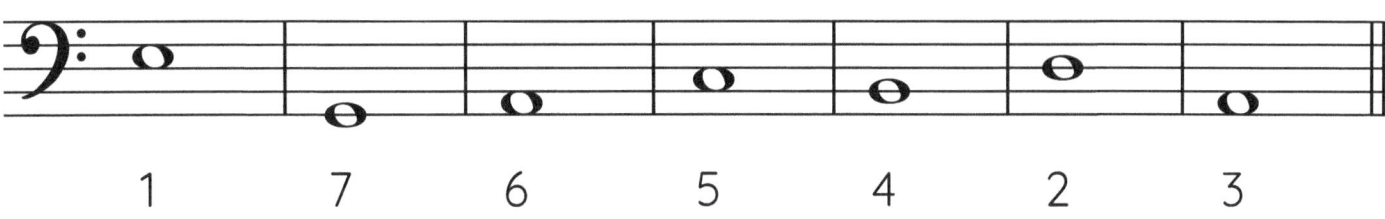

_____
14

WORD SCRAMBLE

Unscramble these words to find Italian musical terms.

largleo __ __ __ __ __ __ __

sifrosmoti __ __ __ __ __ __ __ Ⓞ __

raogl __ __ __ Ⓞ __

aretdoom __ __ __ __ __ __ __

zoemz inpao __ __ Ⓞ __ __   __ __ __ __

troef __ __ __ __ __

niaop __ __ Ⓞ __ __

tendana __ __ __ __ __ __ __

ezmoz rtfeo __ __ __ __   __ __ Ⓞ Ⓞ __

somnisipia __ __ __ __ __ __ __ __ __ __

Copy the circled letters to reveal the hidden word.

__ __ __ __ __ __

50

Pyotr Il'yich Tchaikovsky (1840-1893)

Tchaikovsky was born in Russia. He was composing music even before he began piano lessons at age five. Even so, Tchaikovsky did not choose a music career at first. Instead, he studied law and then worked in the Ministry of Justice in St. Petersburg.

Finally, at age twenty-two, Tchaikovsky gave up his civil service career. He spent the next four years as a student at the St. Petersburg Conservatory. In 1866, he moved to Moscow where he earned a living as a teacher and a music critic.

In 1873, a wealthy woman granted Tchaikovsky an annual allowance so he could devote himself to composition. Tchaikovsky's music has beautiful melodies and brilliant orchestral sounds. His ballets (including the Nutcracker and Swan Lake), his piano concertos, and his violin concerto are frequently performed.

Major Scales

A scale is a series of notes that move up or down by step.

There are many kinds of scales. Each kind of scale has a specific pattern of whole steps and half steps.

The most common scale is the major scale. It consists of:

>two whole steps (W W)
>one half step (H)
>three whole steps (W W W)
>one half step (H)

Here is a simpler way of writing this pattern:

>W W H W W W H

A major scale is named after its starting note. The C major scale begins on C. Let's start on C and follow the pattern for a major scale (W W H W W W H).

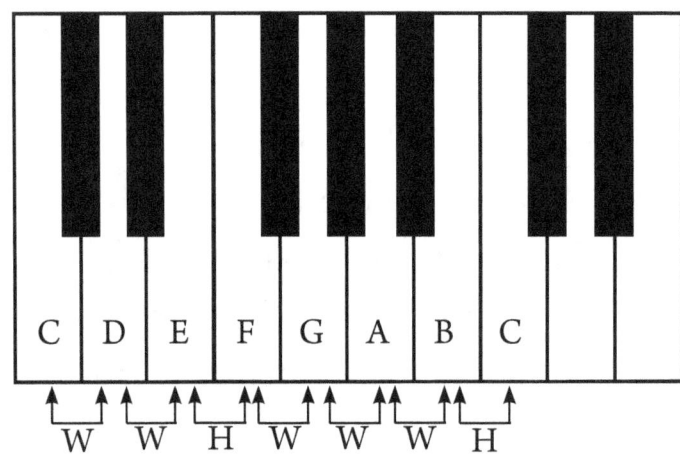

This scale is played on the white keys and it has no sharps or flats.

1. Mark the whole steps (W) and half steps (H) on these C major scales.

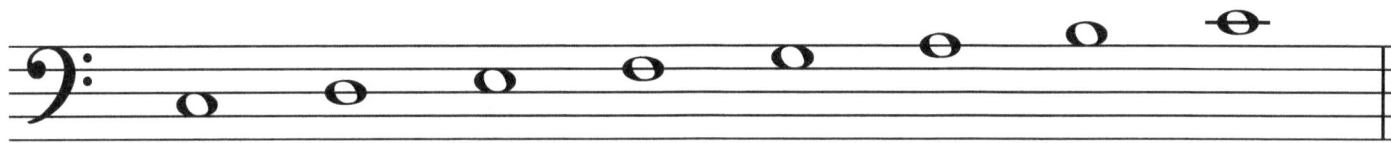

2. Write a C major scale in the treble clef.

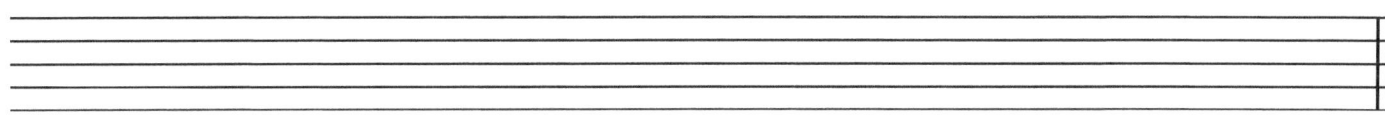

3. Write a C major scale in the bass clef.

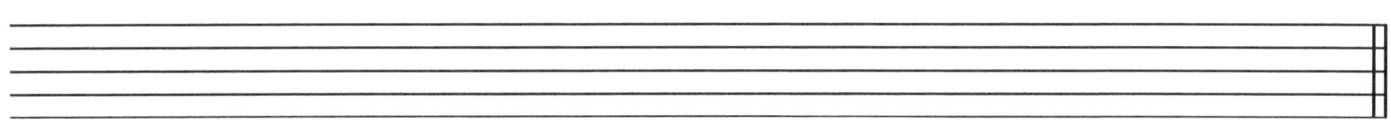

The G Major Scale

When you follow the major scale pattern of whole and half steps starting on G, you get a scale with one sharp. This is the scale of G major.

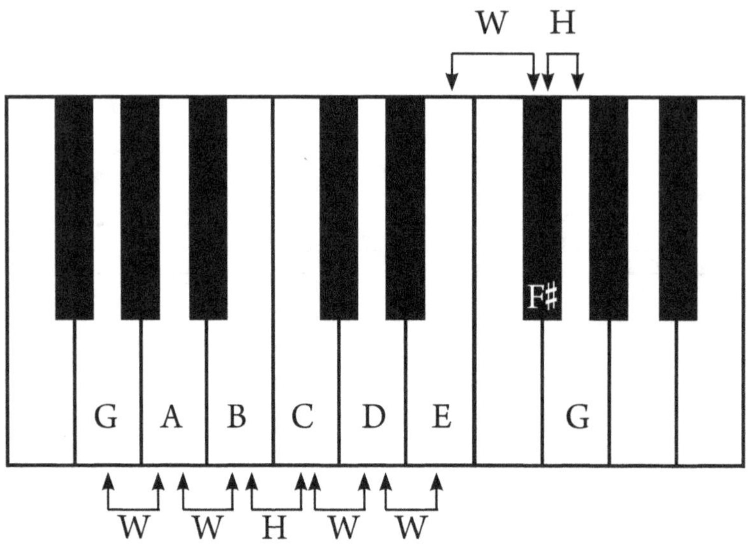

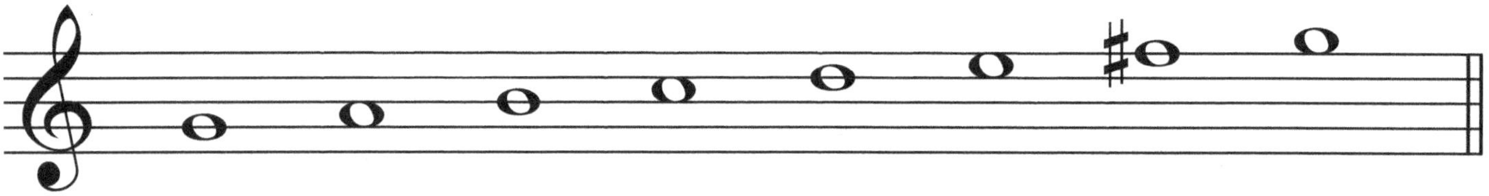

1. Add a sharp to these G major scales, and mark the whole steps (W) and half steps (H).

2. Write a G major scale in the treble clef.

3. Write a G major scale in the bass clef.

Put an X on the key a whole step higher than the key with the ★

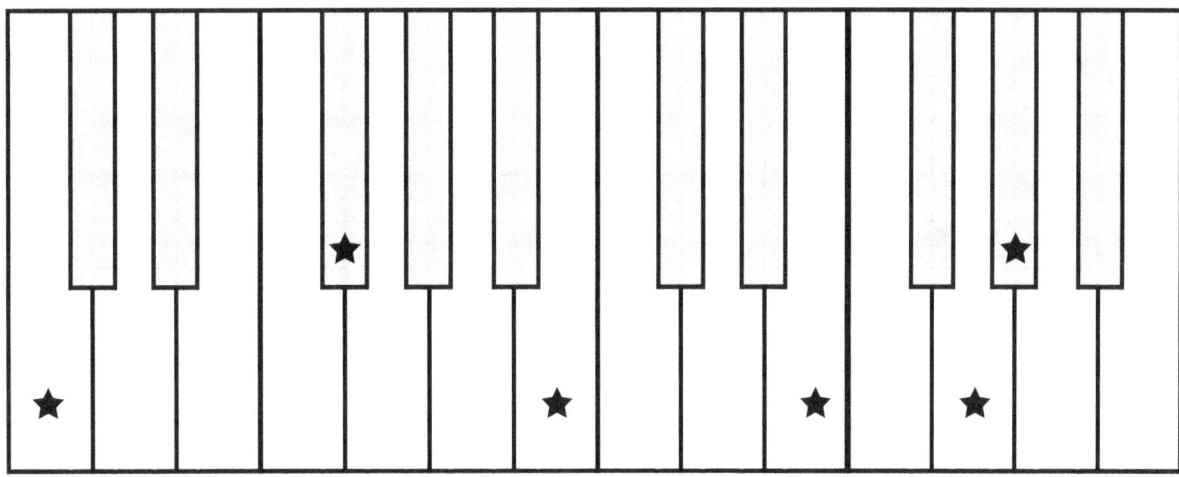

Put an X on the key a whole step lower than the key with the ★

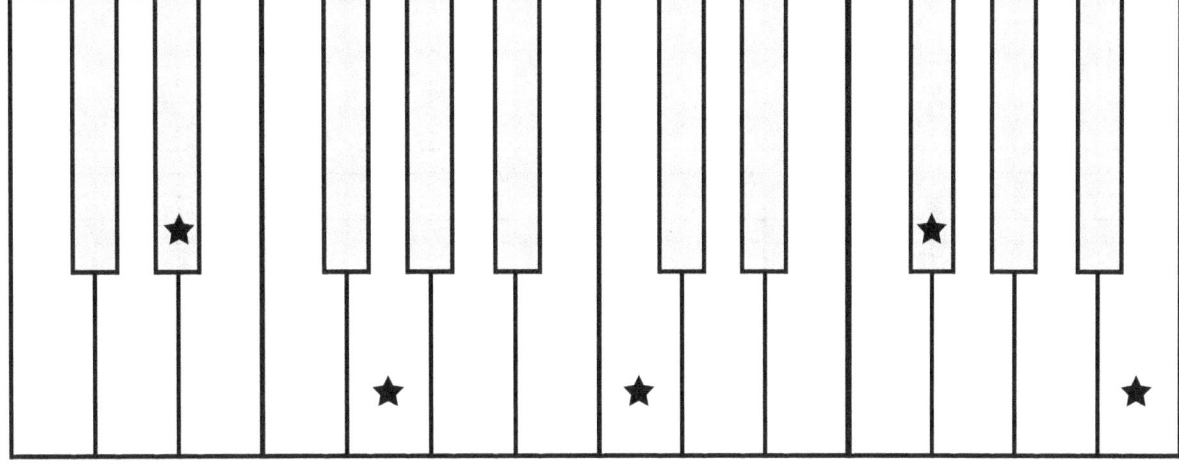

Key Signatures

In both the examples below, there is a sharp on the F line, following the clef at the beginning of the staff.

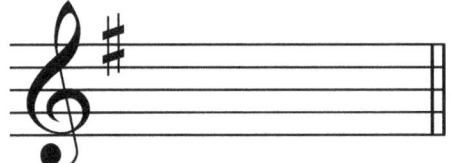 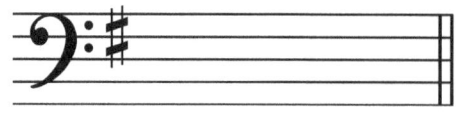

The F sharp tells us that we must play all the Fs sharp.
The sharp in this beginning position is called the key signature.

The G major scale has one sharp: F sharp.

The F sharp in the example above is the key signature of G major. When we use the key signature for G major, we do not have to write a sharp in front of every F.

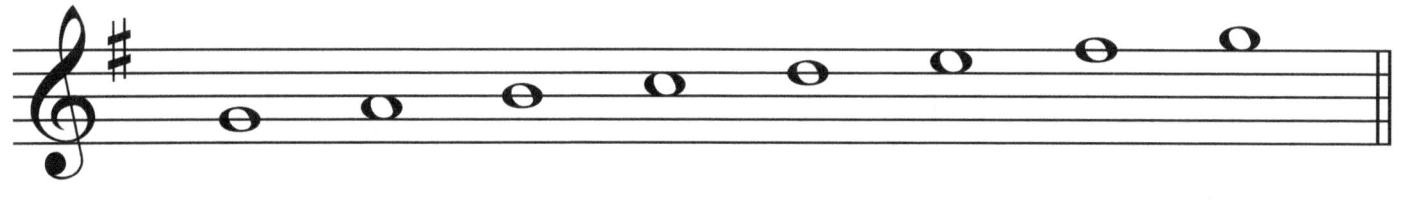

1. Create grand staves and copy the key signature of G major.

2. Write G major scales using a key signature.

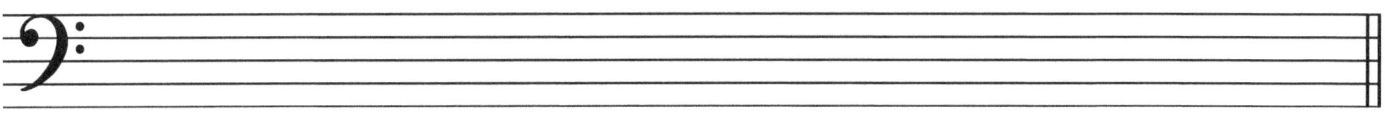

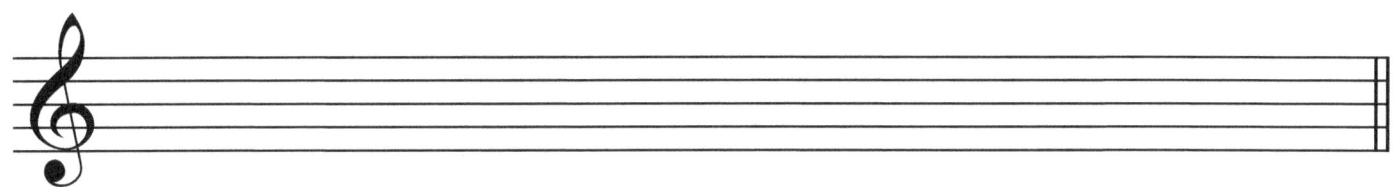

The F Major Scale

When you follow the major scale pattern of whole and half steps starting on F, you get a scale with one flat: B flat. This is the scale of F major.

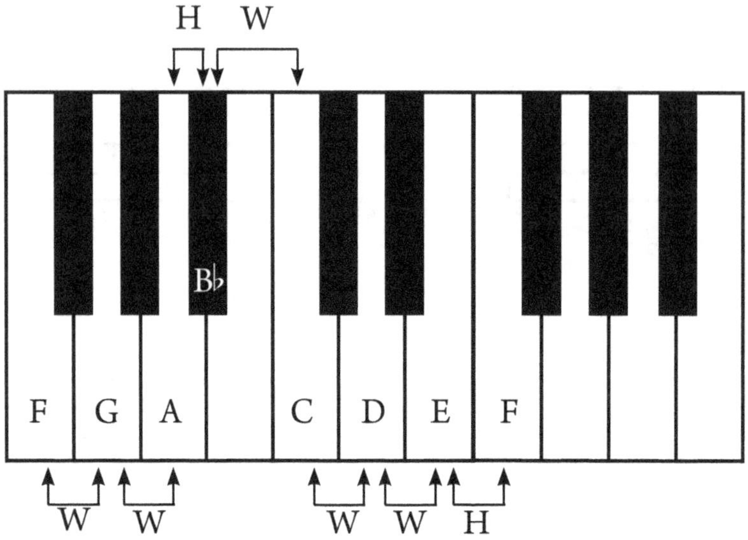

1. Add a flat to these F major scales, and mark the whole steps (W) and half steps (H).

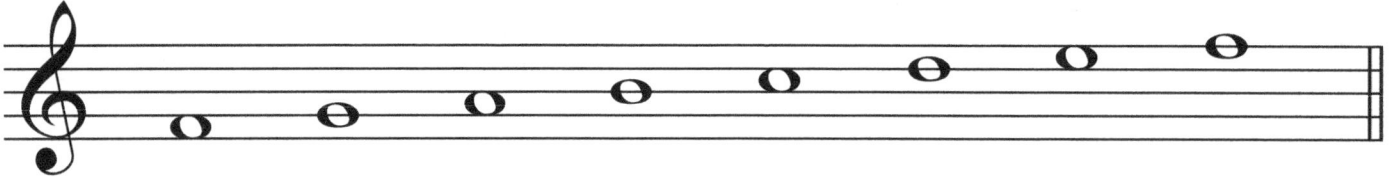

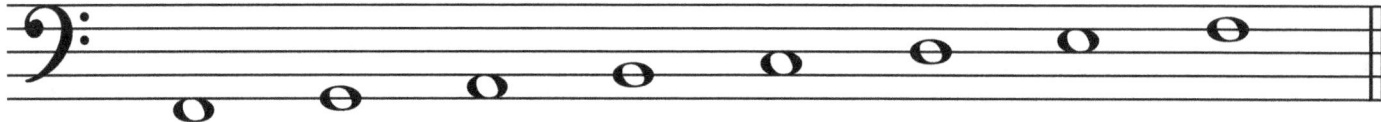

2. Write an F major scale in the treble clef.

3. Write an F major scale in the bass clef.

The Key Signature of F major

In both the examples below, there is a flat on the B line, following the clef at the beginning of the staff.

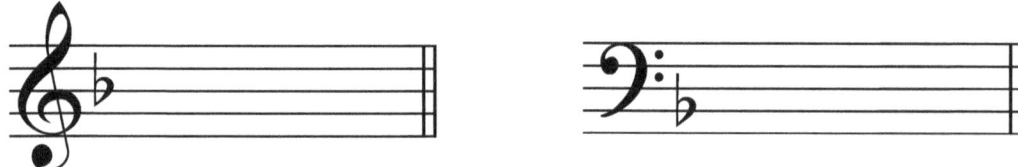

The B flat is a key signature. It tells us we must play all the Bs flat.

The F major scale has one flat: B flat.

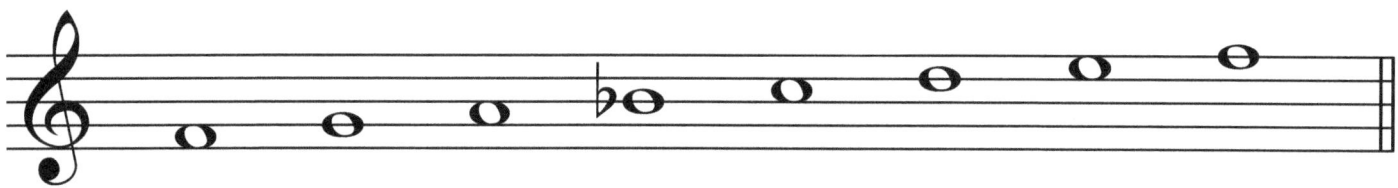

The B flat in the examples above is the key signature of F major. When we use the key signature for F major, we do not have to write a flat in front of every B.

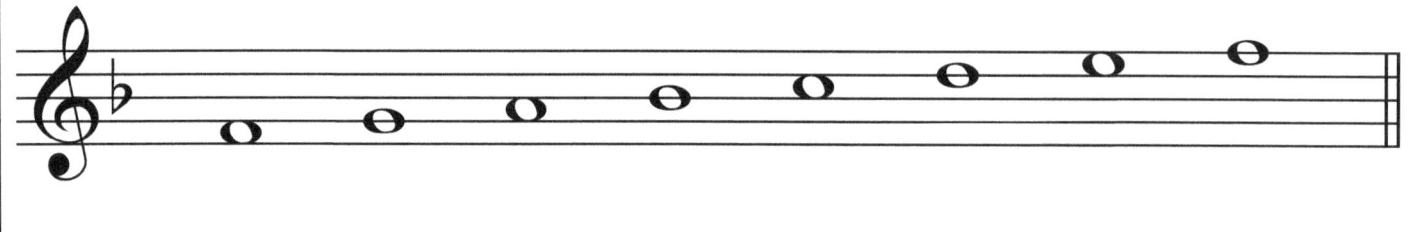

1. Create grand staves and copy the key signature of F major.

2. Write F major scales using a key signature.

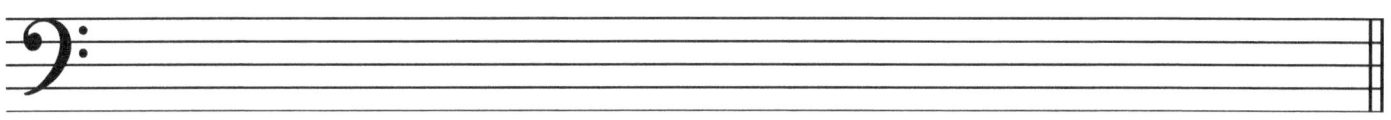

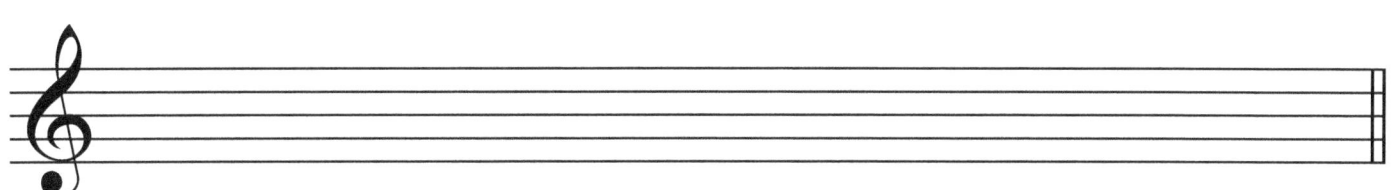

The Scale and Key Signature of D major

When you follow the major scale pattern of whole steps and half steps starting on D, you get a scale with two sharps:
F sharp and C sharp. This is the scale of D major.
The half steps are marked with slurs.

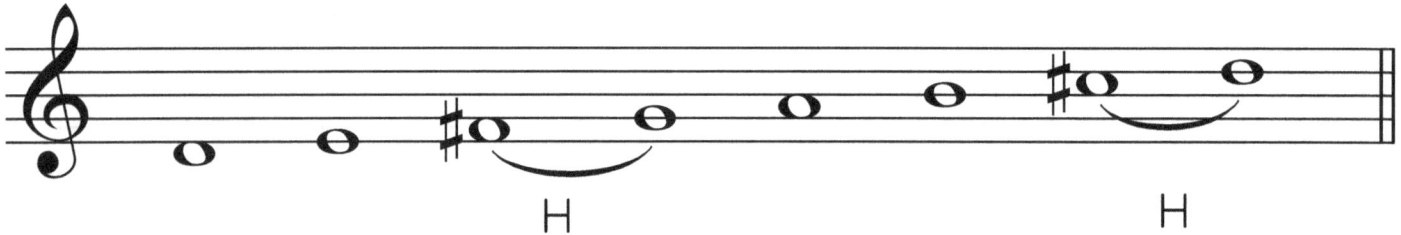

The key signature of D major has two sharps.

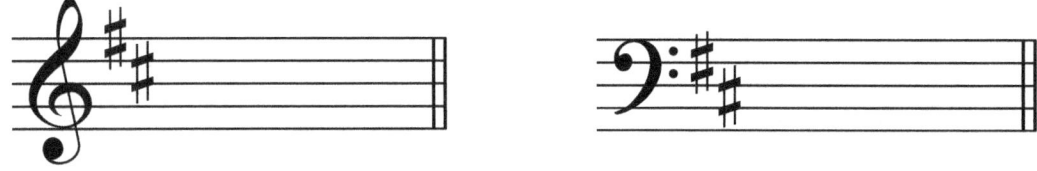

1. Write the D major scale in the treble clef using a key signature. Mark the half steps with slurs.

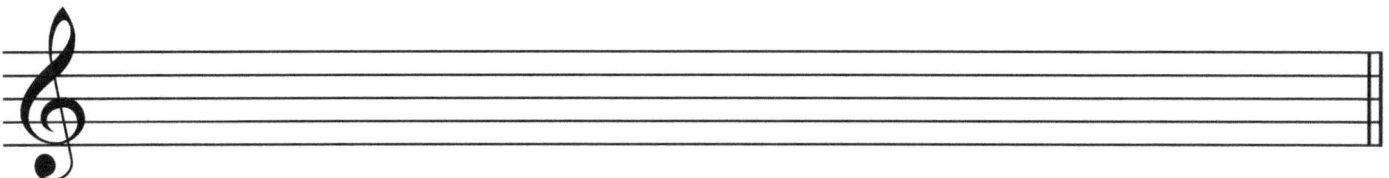

2. Write the D major scale in the bass clef using a key signature. Mark the half steps with slurs.

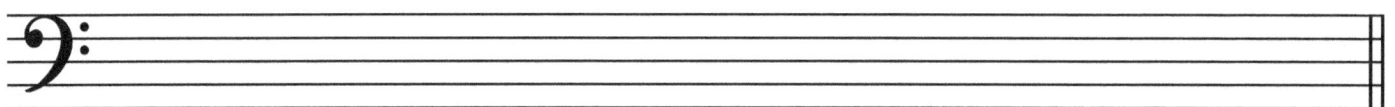

The Scale and Key Signature of B♭ major

When you follow the major scale pattern of whole steps and half steps starting on B flat, you get a scale with two flats:
B flat and E flat. This is the scale of B♭ major.
The half steps are marked with slurs.

The key signature of B flat major has two flats.

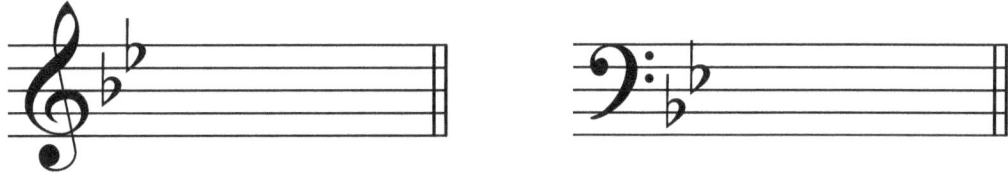

1. Write the B flat major scale in the treble clef using a key signature. Mark the half steps with slurs.

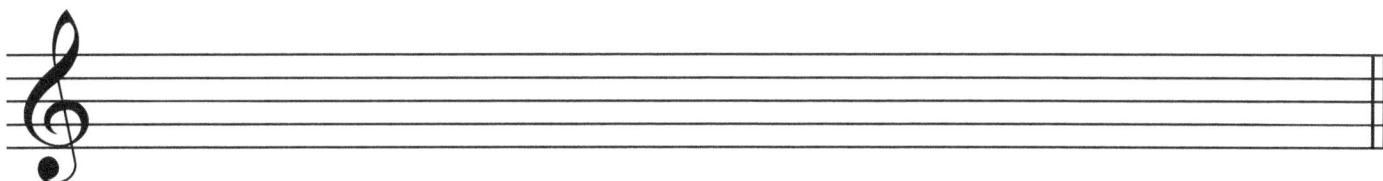

2. Write the B flat major scale in the bass clef using accidentals. Mark the half steps with slurs.

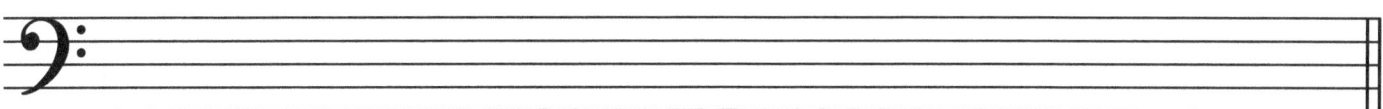

1. Write the following key signatures on the grand staves.

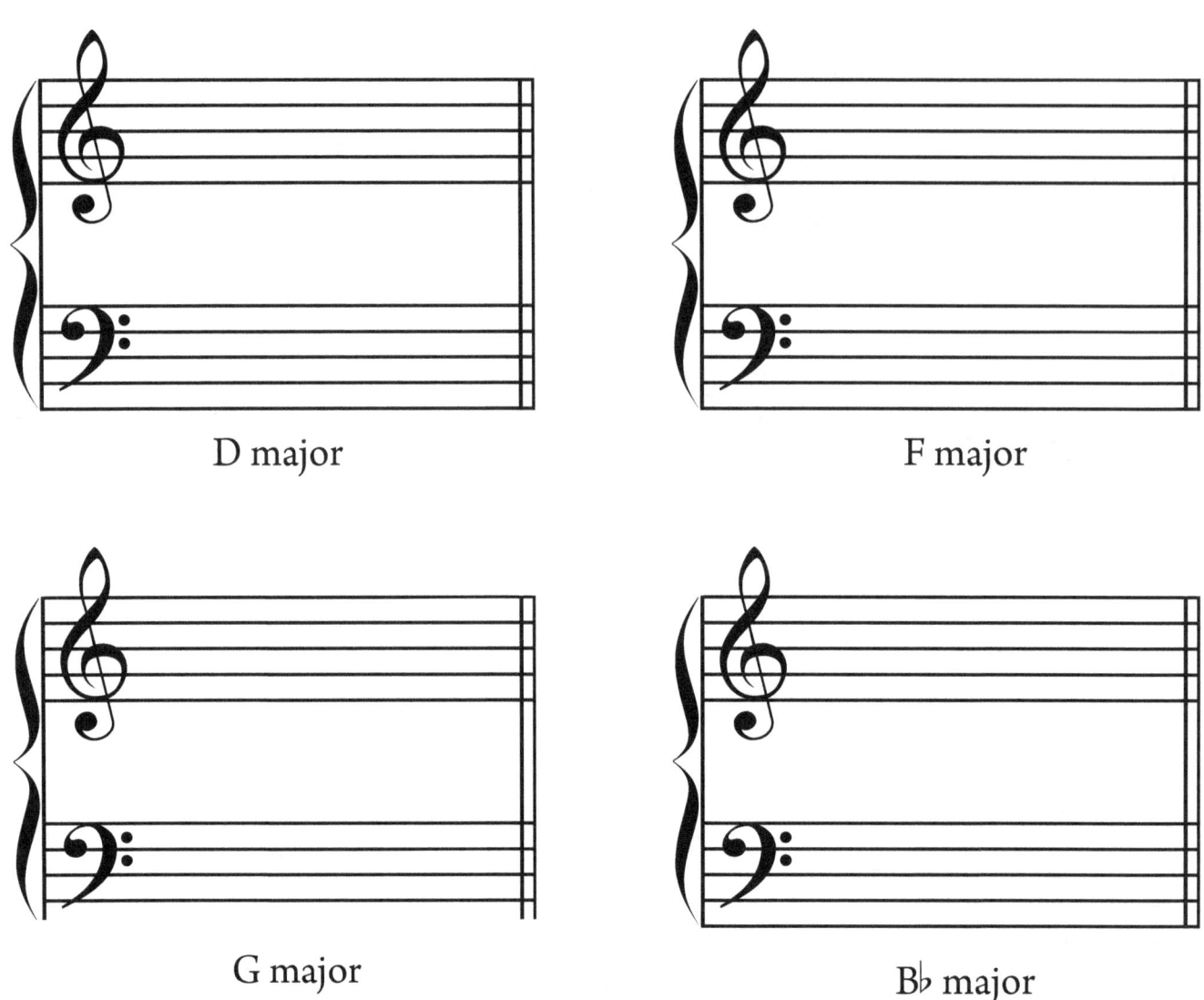

D major

F major

G major

B♭ major

2. Write the following scales using accidentals instead of key signatures. Mark the half steps with slurs.

G major

B♭ major

3. Write the following scales using key signatures. Mark the half steps with slurs.

4. Write the following scales using accidentals instead of key signatures. Mark the half steps with slurs.

MUSICAL WORD SEARCH

Find words from the list below in this puzzle.

```
N R N A T U R A L V
E S E C O N D G W J
O L L M A J O R W S
C V J M E L O D I C
T H V U N I S O N A
A C C I D E N T A L
V F F L A T V Y S E
E B W W S H A R P G
I H A R M O N I C F
B I N T E R V A L N
```

accidental   sharp
flat   harmonic
melodic   interval
scale   unison
second   octave
natural   major

Review Quiz 3

100

1. Add time signatures to the following melodies.

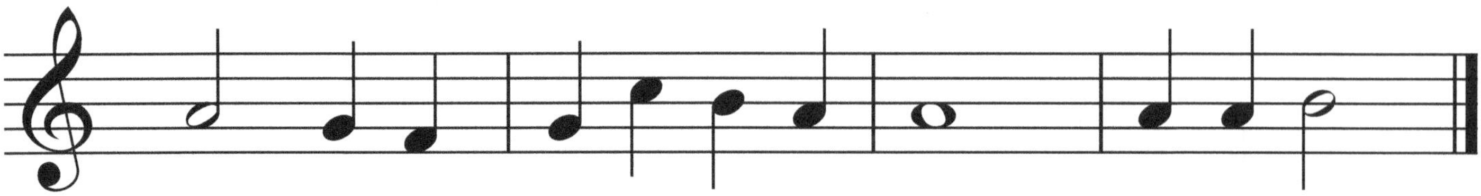

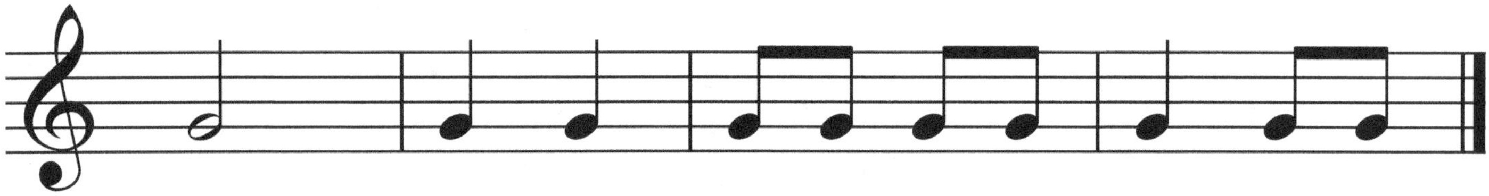

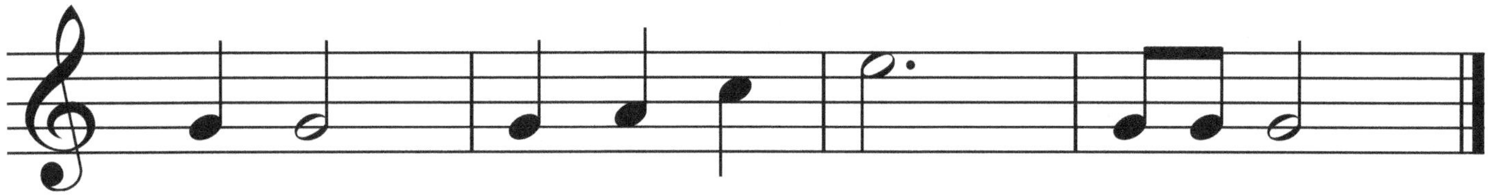

18

2. Add bar lines to the following melodies.

12

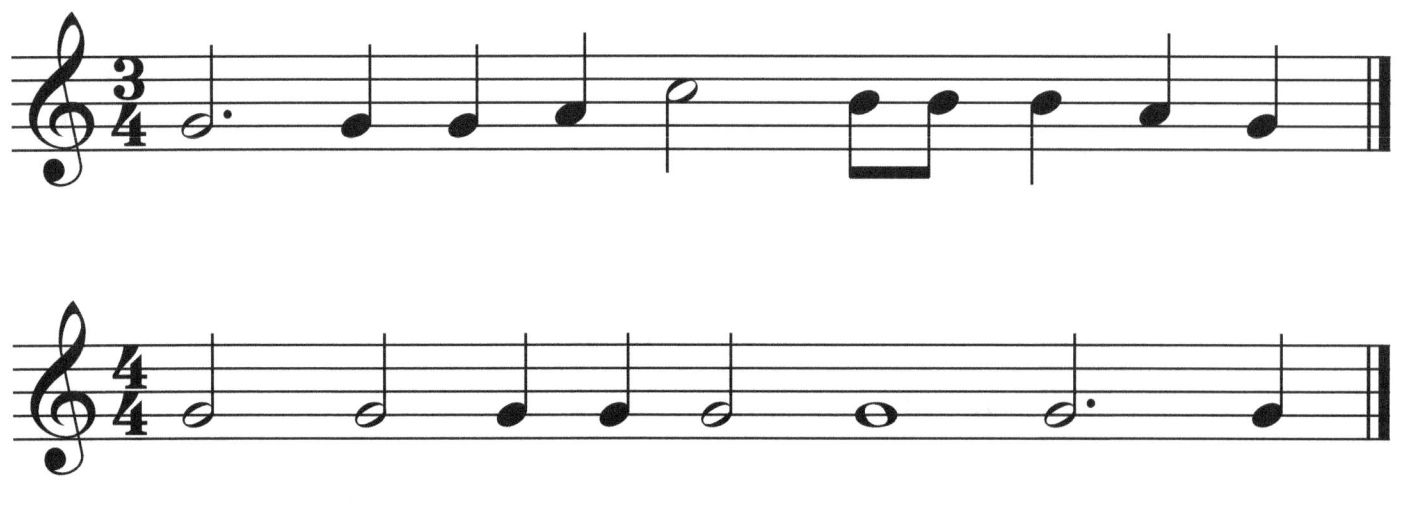

3. Name these notes. Raise them one half step and rename them.

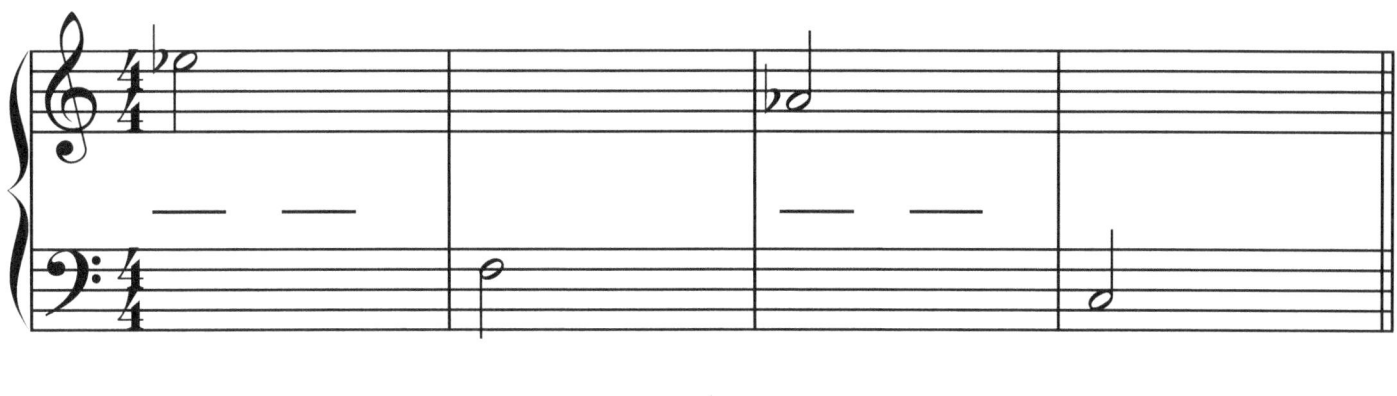

4. Name these notes. Lower them one half step and rename them.

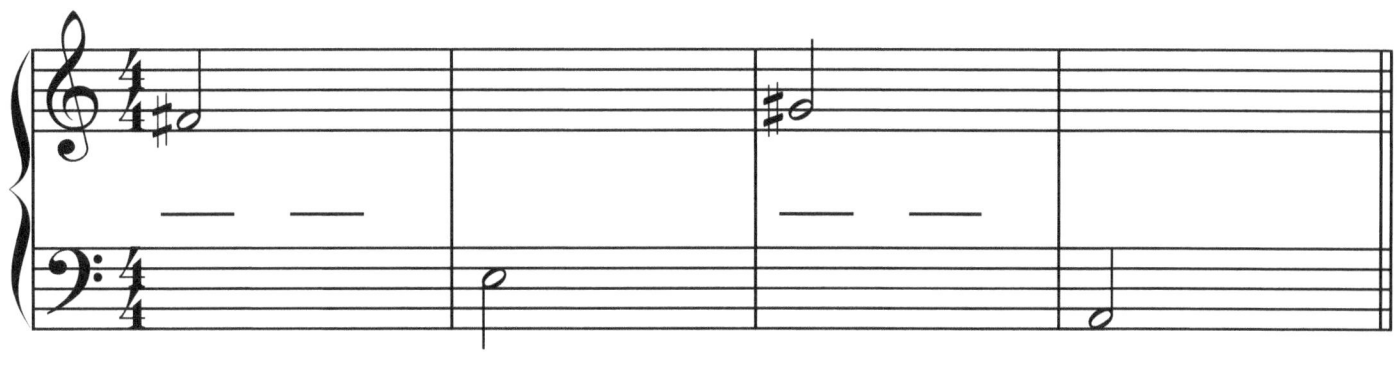

5. Name these intervals.

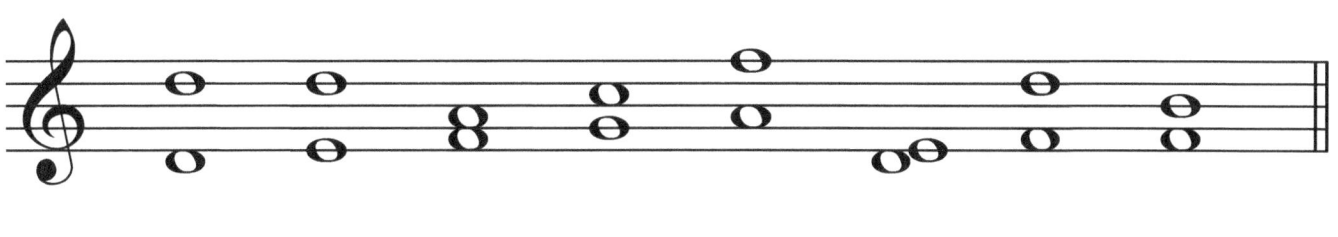

6. Write the following intervals above the given notes.

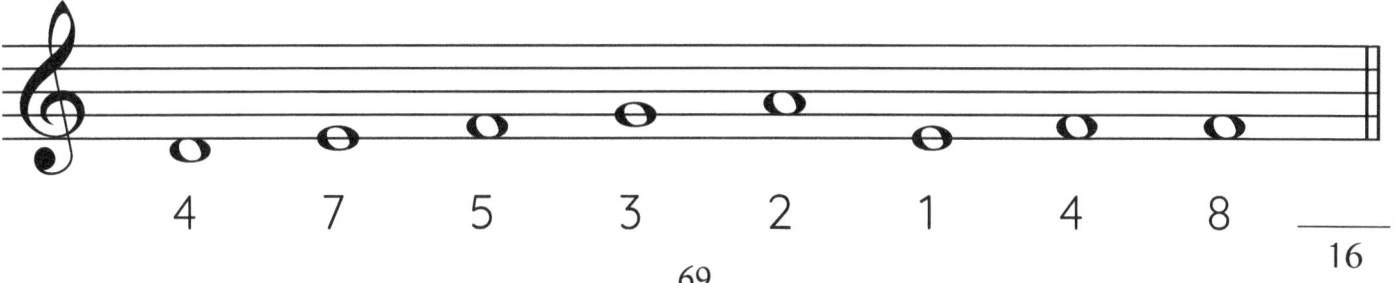

4   7   5   3   2   1   4   8

7. Write these scales using key signatures.

D major

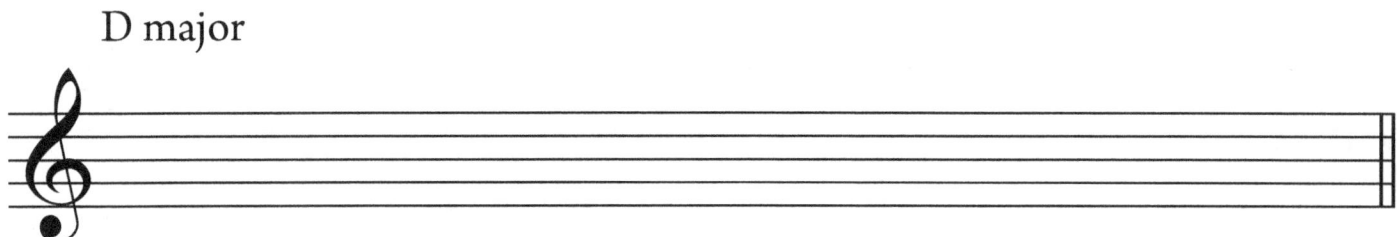

B♭ major

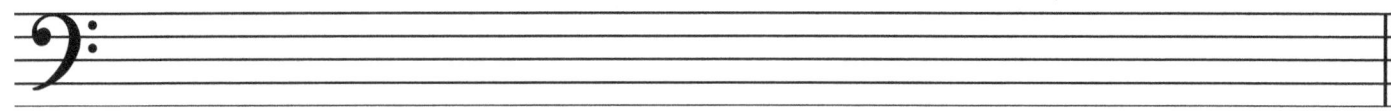

8. Write these scales using accidentals instead of key signatures.

G major

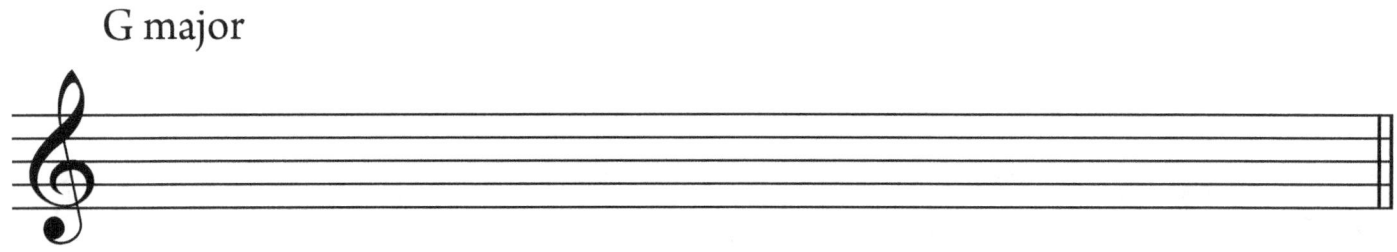

F major

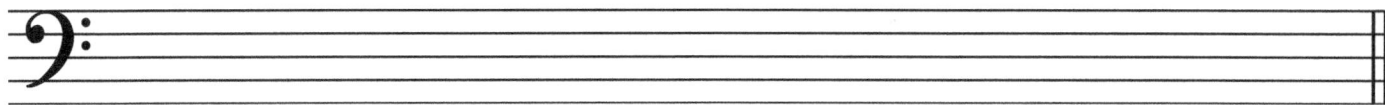

9. Match these terms and signs with their meanings.

mf	very slow
largo	fast
andante	very soft
ff	moderately loud
allegro	moderately slow; walking pace
moderato	at a moderate tempo
pp	very loud

Congratulations! You have finished Book 2! You are now ready to go on to Book 3.

Certificate of Achievement

CONGRATULATIONS TO

_____

You have completed
ELEMENTARY MUSIC THEORY BOOK 2

You are now ready for Elementary Music Theory Book 3

Teacher_____

Date_____

www.ingramcontent.com/pod-product-compliance
Lightning Source LLC
Chambersburg PA
CBHW081711100526
44590CB00022B/3735